C Stephenson
308 Whitman Ct
Buchanan MI 49107-1518

PASSOVER

Your Inspirational Guide

RABBI YECHIEL ECKSTEIN

FOREWORD BY PASTOR GLENN PLUMMER

International Fellowship
of Christians and Jews®

FOREWORD BY PASTOR GLENN PLUMMER

PASSOVER

Your Inspirational Guide

RABBI YECHIEL ECKSTEIN

TABLE of CONTENTS

FOREWORD:
PASTOR GLENN PLUMMER

For more than 3,000 years, the Jewish people have celebrated Passover in obedience to God's command found in Exodus 13:3 (KJV), *"Remember this day, in which ye came out from Egypt, out of the house of bondage; for by strength of hand the LORD brought you out from this place."* Throughout Scripture, the Lord often utilizes commemoration and the establishment of traditions to teach His people. And there are many valuable lessons that the Jewish people have passed on for generations through the Passover observance.

As a Christian pastor, I, too, have found joy and great wisdom from studying the Exodus story. Most especially, I have found the deep understanding that we serve a God whom we can fully depend upon. He is a merciful, Heavenly Father who hears the cries of His people and responds to our needs. Like most pastors, I regularly preach from this passage of Scripture. But several years ago, when I attended my first *Seder* hosted by an Orthodox rabbi and his family, my understanding of this biblically ordained commemoration and tradition was deepened in a way that is difficult to put into words. Found within the Passover tradition as commemorated in Judaism are concrete and vivid lessons that one can hear, see, taste, and smell at the *seder* table — lessons forged in the suffering of humanity and experienced in the glorious freedom that comes from our faith in a loving, merciful, and Almighty God.

In these pages, you will learn what I discovered firsthand at the *seder* table. I am indebted to my dear friend Rabbi Yechiel Eckstein, who taught me the deep and historic lessons rooted in thousands of years of tradition and faithfulness by the Jewish people that have been passed down from one generation to the next as the Lord instructed in Deuteronomy 6:4 (KJV), *"And thou shalt teach them diligently unto thy children . . ."* Just think of that! God *has been* faithful, *is* faithful, and *will be* faithful to His children. True freedom for our souls is discovered through our obedience to His Word and instructions for our lives. As you read through this inspirational guide and glean these truths, we should also pause and thank God for the faithfulness of His children — the Jewish people — for how He has used them to teach us His ways.

It is my prayer that your understanding of the God whom we serve — the God of Abraham, Isaac, and Jacob, the mighty God of Israel — will be deepened as you delve into the history and traditions of the Passover celebration. That through this understanding you will taste of His goodness, you will see that He can be trusted, you will smell the sweet aroma of His unfailing love for His people, and you will experience His unfailing grace and mercy all the days of your life.

Now come, let us explore the deep Jewish roots of our faith through the Passover tradition.

Dr. Glenn Plummer
Sr. Pastor, Ambassadors for Christ Church
Detroit, Michigan
Jurisdictional Overseer for the State of Israel
Church of God in Christ

INTRODUCTION

On that day tell your son, "I do this because of what the LORD did for me when I came out of Egypt." — EXODUS 13:8

This book that you hold in your hands represents thousands of years of Jewish tradition. In all of human history, the Exodus has been the most influential event in shaping both Jewish history and civilization as we know it. From that very first *seder* meal on the eve of the Exodus, when the Israelites first sacrificed the Passover lamb, until the commemorative Passover meal we observe today, this ancient celebration continues to remind us that there is a God, a God Who hears our cries, creates miracles, and brings about salvation.

Inside this book, you will find an overview and explanation of how the Jewish people have observed Passover for thousands of years. We have also provided a devotional guide for inspirational reading during the Passover season. In the third section, you will find the traditional text of the *haggadah*, the guide that takes us through our commemorative meal, the *Seder*, on Passover night. We have included commentary in order to explain and expound upon the text that tells the Exodus story. In Exodus 13:8, God instructs us, "*V'higaddita,*" to tell the story of Passover, and from that first Passover onward, the children of Israel have done just that with the guidance of the *haggadah*.

The first official *haggadah* wasn't committed to writing until the first century C.E., just after the destruction of the Second Temple in Jerusalem. However, we know that at least part of the liturgy goes back even further than that time period. For example, Judaism's oral tradition teaches that the time-honored "Four Questions" that serve as a focal part of the Passover *Seder* today are a modified set of four questions that were asked during Temple times when the Passover sacrifice was still offered. Over the centuries, the *haggadah* has been adapted to fit the times, augmented and elaborated upon. It is a living guide, one that attests to the life of a nation and a people through the generations.

The *haggadah* that Jews all over the world use today is overwhelmingly composed from the *haggadah* that was solidified in the late 1400s. Since then, there have been minor modifications and hundreds of commentaries. Yet, in every *haggadah*, no matter the theme or tradition, the central message remains the same as it did on the very first Passover night.

This particular *haggadah* was created in order to share with you, our Christian friends – many of whom are interested in knowing more about the Jewish roots of the Christian faith— the beauty and significance of the Passover customs and traditions observed today. It is a celebration that honors the Exodus story and brings it into our lives. For both Christians and Jews alike, the Exodus story is the foundation of our faith and the cornerstone of our hope that the ultimate redemption will soon be at hand. It is also a springboard for thanksgiving and praising God for the many miracles in our lives.

In Judaism, we recite a blessing before performing any one of God's commandments. Telling the story of Passover is one of those divine directives; however, it is an exception to the rule. There is no blessing recited before telling the Passover story. In questioning why, the Jewish sages respond that the reason why we don't recite a blessing before performing this specific commandment is because it is one that has no beginning and has no end.

In Jewish prayers we recognize that there is no end to praising God and thanking Him for His countless miracles in our lives. We say:

"Were our mouths as full of song as the sea, and our tongues as full of joyous song as its multitude of waves, and our lips as full of praise as the breadth of the heavens, and our eyes as brilliant as the sun and the moon, and our hands as outspread as the eagles of the sky and our feet as swift as hinds — we still could not thank You sufficiently, LORD our God and God of our forefathers, and to bless Your Name for even one of the thousand thousand, thousands of thousands and myriad myriads of favors, miracles, and wonders that you performed for our ancestors and for us."

We can never fully express our gratitude to our God and Savior, but with this *haggadah*, we shall offer our best.

It is my hope and prayer that you will be blessed by a greater understanding of this biblically mandated tradition that has been handed down from generation to generation for thousands of years. May you, too, grow in your faith and your walk with the Almighty One as you fathom the deep, deep roots of your faith.

Rabbi Eckstein

THE OVERVIEW

PASSOVER — A LASTING ORDINANCE

"This is a day you are to commemorate; for the generations to come you shall celebrate it as a festival to the LORD—a lasting ordinance." — EXODUS 12:14

photo credit-Philip Bird LRPS CPAGB

Famed musician and teacher Rabbi Shlomo Carlebach shared the following story about the last Passover in the Warsaw ghetto during the darkest days of the Holocaust in 1943. Only one Jewish family with one child, Moishele, remained in the ghetto. According to custom, the child asked his father the traditional Four Questions on Passover night. When Moishele finished asking the questions, he said, "Father, I have a question of my own."

"Go ahead and ask, my son," the father replied.

The boy began, "Father, will you be alive next year to answer my questions?" He continued,

"Will I be alive next year to ask you the questions?" Then, "Will there be any Jewish child left in the whole world next year to ask the Four Questions on Passover night?"

The father was heartbroken, but with great faith, he answered, "The truth is, my dear child, I don't know. I don't know if I will be alive next year, and I don't know if you will be alive next year. But I do know that there will always be one child somewhere in the world who will ask the Four Questions on Passover night. For the Lord our God has promised it."

———— ✦ ————

And so it has been over the past three thousand years. Passover has endured as the most celebrated and widely observed holiday in the Jewish tradition. Despite centuries of persecution and exile, the *seder* night has remained sacred for the Jewish people. Even during the bleakest chapter in Jewish history, the Holocaust, countless stories are told of Jews in Nazi death camps who struggled to commemorate the Passover in some small way, even as their observance risked certain death. In the most far-flung Jewish communities around the world, traditions may vary, but the importance of this night remains the same. Today, the overwhelming majority of Jews attend a Passover *Seder*, even if it is the only Jewish practice that they observe all year. And recently, many Christians have begun participating in this time-honored tradition, as they, too, reaffirm the shared values and beliefs that are recounted on *seder* night.

THE SIGNIFICANCE OF PASSOVER

"Commemorate this day, the day you came out of Egypt, out of the land of slavery, because the LORD brought you out of it with a mighty hand." — EXODUS 13:3

Why is this holiday of all holidays so sacred?

The answer is because Passover commemorates the seminal event in Jewish history. The story of the Exodus, around which the holiday is focused, recalls the birth of the Jewish nation,

Israel. In addition, from the lessons learned and themes woven into this timeless story are drawn the most basic and fundamental principles found in Judaism. The suffering of the children of Israel and their deliverance from slavery reaffirms our faith that the Lord our God cares about His people, that He hears our prayers, and most importantly, that He intervenes in human history in order to bring about salvation so that we may serve and worship Him.

These core values — faith, prayer, deliverance, freedom, and service to God — are so foundational that God commanded us to commemorate Passover every year for seven days (outside of Israel, eight). Once a year, we devote an entire week to recalling the events of the Exodus and internalizing their messages.

In addition, we remember the Exodus every week on the Sabbath. Scripture reads: *"Remember that you were slaves in Egypt and that the LORD your God brought you out of there with a mighty hand and an outstretched arm. Therefore the LORD your God*

has commanded you to observe the Sabbath day" (Deuteronomy 5:15). As we rest and serve God on the Sabbath every week, we are reminded that we can only do so because we are free. God's salvation and deliverance is a gift that we honor weekly.

If that were not enough, we are also commanded to remember the Exodus story every day: *"...all the days of your life you may remember the time of your departure from Egypt"* (Deuteronomy 16:3). Jews fulfill this biblical

Crossing the Red Sea

injunction through various daily practices such as donning a *tallit*, a prayer shawl with tassels described by Scripture: *"...you are to make tassels on the corners of your garments"* (Numbers 15:38). The *tallit* is a reminder of God's salvation, *"Then you will remember to obey all my commands. . . . I am the LORD your God, who brought you out of Egypt"* (Numbers 15:40–41). Additionally, both the section in the book of Exodus that commands us to remember the Exodus story and the portion that directs us to tell the story to our children, constitute two of four biblical texts placed in the two boxes of *tefillin*, or phylacteries, which are worn on observant Jews' heads during worship. The story of the Exodus also features prominently in the daily prayer service; the entire Song of the Sea, which celebrates the Israelites' miraculous deliverance from the Egyptian army (Exodus 15:1–18), is included in morning prayers. The Exodus is a focal point in Judaism's two most sacred prayers — the *Shema* and the *Amidah*, which are recited several times each day. In addition, the Exodus story is the basis for many social biblical directives such as giving charity to the poor and taking care of the convert, the widow, and the orphan.

The story of the Exodus is the rock upon which Judaism stands. If Judaism serves as the root of Christianity, then it is Passover and the Exodus that nourish the roots of us all.

THE EXODUS STORY

Then the LORD said to him, "Know for certain that for four hundred years your descendants will be strangers in a country not their own and that they will be enslaved and mistreated there. But I will punish the nation they serve as slaves, and afterward they will come out with great possessions." — GENESIS 15:13–14

The Exodus story, which is well-known to both Jews and Christians, actually begins in the book of Genesis with God's promise to Abraham as he entered into a covenant with God. In Genesis 15:13–16, God told Abraham that his descendants would be enslaved in a foreign land for four hundred years, but that they

Joseph Sold by His Brethren, *by Gustave Doré*

would be redeemed and returned to the land given to Abraham. This promise set the blueprint for the next few centuries as Abraham and Sarah gave birth to Isaac; Isaac, in turn, had a son, Jacob, who had twelve sons. Because Jacob's sons were jealous of their younger brother Joseph, their father's favorite, they sold him to a group of traders who eventually sold him to a master in Egypt. Through a series of circumstances that only God could have orchestrated, Joseph ultimately became the Prime Minister of Egypt, in charge of overseeing the storage of grain gathered during the abundant years so that the country would survive the coming years of famine — events that Joseph foretold by interpreting the Pharaoh's dreams. During those years of famine, Joseph's eleven brothers and their father, Jacob, traveled to Egypt to find food and were reunited with Joseph. Together, they settled in Egypt, raising their families and growing in numbers.

All this, of course, is the prologue to the heart of the Exodus story, but it is recounted on Passover in order to emphasize that God was at work throughout the centuries to set the stage for the scenes to unfold in exactly the right way at the right time.

The story picks up several generations later after the twelve tribes of Israel had settled in Egypt when a new Pharaoh took the throne *"to whom Joseph meant nothing"* (Exodus 1:8). This Pharaoh, concerned about the growing number of Israelites in his land, decreed that all Jewish baby boys be killed at birth. To further ensure that the Hebrews would not pose any threat, he enslaved the children of Israel. Hundreds of years passed in bitter slavery. The Israelites increased in number as their hardships and sorrows multiplied as well. Scripture now turns to the story of Moses, who as a baby was saved from Pharaoh's evil decree by being placed in a basket and set in the Nile River, ending up in the hands of Pharaoh's daughter. Moses was brought up in Pharaoh's palace as an Egyptian prince, but was forced to leave when he killed an

The First Passover

Egyptian whom he witnessed beating an Israelite slave. Taking refuge in the desert of Midian, Moses encountered God in a burning bush. The time for the Israelites' deliverance was at hand. God commanded Moses to deliver His people from slavery, sending him to Pharaoh with the directive: *"Let my people go"* (Exodus 5:1).

When Pharaoh repeatedly refused Moses' request, God unleashed nine terrible plagues that struck Egypt and her people. Yet, Pharaoh remained stubborn and hard-hearted until God sent a tenth and final horrific plague — the death of all firstborn sons throughout Egypt. Only the Israelites, who in obedience to God's instructions placed the blood of a lamb on the doorposts of their homes, were spared as God's angel of death passed over them. Finally, Pharaoh, who had lost his own son to the deadly plague, relented and the Israelites were freed. Yet, even before the Israelites could safely leave the country, Pharaoh changed his mind and sent his army after the children of Israel. Caught between the Red Sea and the quickly approaching Egyptian army, the people cried out to God, who instructed them to walk into the sea. As they walked forward in faith, the sea parted, but only for enough time to allow the Israelites to safely pass through. As the Egyptian army followed in full pursuit, the waves crashed down on them, wiping out the entire Egyptian army and effectively destroying what was left of the Egyptian empire.

These are the events and miracles remembered and retold on the *seder* night. But they are not the end of the story. The story continues as the children of Israel, now freed, were led to Mount Sinai, where they received the Ten Commandments and the *Torah* from God. This, perhaps, is the most important part of the Exodus story because it teaches us that with the privilege of freedom comes the responsibility of service. Scripture makes this connection when describing God's words to the children of Israel at Mount Sinai: *"You yourselves have seen what I did to Egypt, and how I carried you on eagles' wings and brought you to myself. Now if you obey me fully and keep my covenant, then out of all nations you will be my treasured possession"* (Exodus 19:4–5). God freed the Israelites so that they may be obedient servants to Him — because it is only in service to God that a person can be truly free.

As we recount the Exodus story each Passover during the *Seder*, we confirm as a people where we came from, who we are, and what we stand for. We reaffirm our national identity and our shared mission.

THE NAMES OF PASSOVER

"The blood will be a sign for you on the houses where you are, and when I see the blood, I will pass over you. No destructive plague will touch you when I strike Egypt." — EXODUS 12:13

Passover is known by four different names, each of which alludes to a different aspect of the essence of the holiday. From each name we learn more about the meaning of the holiday and what we are celebrating.

The most common of these names is *Pesach*, the Hebrew word for Passover, which has a double meaning. First, it is mentioned in relation to the lamb that the children of Israel were commanded to sacrifice to the Lord on the eve of the Exodus. With shoes on and staff in hand, they were required to *"Eat it in haste; it is the LORD's Passover"* (Exodus 12:11). Secondly, the word refers to God's angel of death passing over the houses of the Israelites. Sheep were considered gods in ancient Egypt; therefore, God commanded the Israelites to demonstrate their faith in Him by slaughtering these false deities and placing the blood of the lamb on the doorposts of their homes for all Egypt to see. This would be a sign to God who would then "pass over" these Jewish homes during the plague that killed all firstborn Egyptians.

However, in most places where Passover is mentioned in the Bible, Scripture opts for a different name — *Chag Ha'Matzot*, The Festival of Unleavened Bread: *"Celebrate the Festival of Unleavened Bread, because it was on this very day that I brought your divisions out of Egypt"* (Exodus 12:17). Unleavened bread, more commonly known as *matzah*, was

Bound Lamb *or* Agnus Dei, *1630s by Francisco de Zurbarán*

the bread the Israelites ate on their way out of Egypt. There was not enough time for the dough to rise, so they cooked flatbread and left Egypt for the unknown. *Matzah* became a symbol of Passover and a reminder of the trust that the children of Israel had in God. Because of that symbolism, the Jewish sages have another name for *matzah* — "the bread of faith."

Rabbi Levi Yitzchak of Berditchev, a Hasidic Master during the eighteenth century, provides us with a beautiful explanation for why we call the holiday *Pesach* or Passover, and in the Bible, God calls it the Festival of Unleavened Bread. He taught that God and the Jewish people each refer to the holiday with the name that best expresses each other's faithfulness, love, and greatness. We highlight the fact that God spared the firstborn of the children of Israel, acknowledging His great love and faithfulness. However, God emphasizes the great faith and trust that the Israelites had in Him when they left the comfort and security of their homes in order to follow Him into the desert: *"...how as a bride you loved me and followed me through the wilderness"* (Jeremiah 2:2). The Israelites' faithfulness is symbolized by the *matzah*, giving the holiday its biblical name.

A third name for Passover is *Chag Ha'Aviv*, the Holiday of Spring. Scripture tells us, *"Observe the month of Aviv and celebrate the Passover of the LORD your God, because in the month of Aviv he brought you out of Egypt by night"* (Deuteronomy 16:1). Spring is a time of renewal and rejuvenation. After the long imprisonment of winter that restricts growth, spring ushers in a time for new life to come forth. Flowers blossom and bloom as nature comes back to life and thrives once again. As we read in Song of Songs: *"See! The winter is past; the rains are over and gone. Flowers appear on the earth; the season of singing has come"* (2:11–12). By calling Passover by the name of spring, we make the connection between the liberation of the Israelites from Egypt and the budding of flowers, between the Song of the Sea that the Israelites sang after they witnessed the great miracle and the *"season of singing."* Egypt symbolizes a long cold winter season; the Exodus represents the spring of the Jewish nation — a time for freedom in order to blossom, grow, and thrive again.

Finally, Passover is also referred to as *Z'man Cheirutainu*, the Time of Our Freedom. The sages explain that every holiday on the Jewish calendar has a specific spiritual energy that is present during that observance every year. For example, *Yom Kippur* is a time of forgiveness, *Hanukkah* a time of miracles. Passover is a time of freedom because each year during this holiday the potential for freedom and liberation is the greatest. According to this understanding, all the ideas behind the different names of Passover – faith, salvation, freedom, and growth – are most accessible to each of us at this time every year.

CELEBRATING PASSOVER

"You must keep this ordinance at the appointed time year after year." — EXODUS 13:10

In order to fulfill the biblical injunction to observe the Passover every year, there are several rituals that we follow even today. In biblical times when the Holy Temple stood in Jerusalem, a Passover sacrifice was required, recalling the original lamb sacrificed on the eve of the Exodus. While the Temple no longer stands today and sacrifices are no longer offered, we still are able to celebrate Passover through

observing and following the other commandments in the Bible.

The most notable aspect of the Passover observances today is eating the flat, cracker-like bread that we call *matzah*. Scripture dictates, *"Eat unleavened bread during those seven days; nothing with yeast in it is to be seen among you, nor shall any yeast be seen anywhere within your borders"* (Exodus 13:7). Not only are we to eat *matzah*, but we are also to rid our homes of any products containing yeast, which we do not consume for the duration of Passover. In addition, the first and last days (first two days and last two days outside of Israel) are observed as *"a sacred assembly"* where we *"do no work at all"* (Exodus 12:16). Like the Sabbath, these days are designated as holy days on which we do nothing but worship God and spend time with family and friends in the spirit of the holiday.

The highlight of the Passover experience and observance is the traditional *Seder*, which is held on the first night of Passover (first two nights outside of Israel) and during which the Exodus

Passover, engraving published 1670 by Gerard Jollain

story is told. The Bible includes numerous directives to tell the Passover story *"that you may tell your children and grandchildren how I dealt harshly with the Egyptians and how I performed my signs among them, and that you may know that I am the LORD"* (Exodus 10:2). Essential to the Passover celebration is remembering our past and passing on our legacy to future generations. In fact, a two-word homonym for the word *Pesach* is the Hebrew words *peh* and *sach*, which

mean "the mouth speaks." Speaking and telling our story is an integral part of observing *Pesach*.

Traditionally, we tell the Passover story at a *Seder* using a *haggadah*, or guide. The word *seder* means "order." It sets the stage for the night by outlining fifteen steps in a specific order that take us through the Passover story and help us integrate the messages through various rituals, Scriptures, and prayers. The *haggadah* is a book that serves as our script for the night. The word *haggadah* is related to the word *le'haggid*, which means "to tell." Therefore, the *haggadah* is our guide to the *Seder* that helps us tell the Exodus story.

In the words of the *haggadah*, "Every person must see himself or herself as personally having left Egypt." The goal of the *Seder* is to help us literally experience the Exodus so that we can fully internalize its meaning. It is for this reason that the *Seder* is intended to be completely hands-on and interactive. In some homes, the *Seder* begins with the leader entering the room dressed as an ancient Israelite carrying *matzah* on his shoulder. The guests ask, "Where have you come from?" To which the leader replies, "I have come from Egypt." Then the guests ask, "And where are you going?" The leader says, "I am going to Jerusalem." Judaism couples words with actions throughout the night in order to make the ideas of the Bible real and help us integrate them on a deep and personal level.

At the heart of the *Seder* is asking questions. Participation is encouraged, so instead of the leader speaking the entire night, guests are encouraged to participate both through sharing the readings and by asking questions. In particular, we focus on inspiring our children to ask questions, as ultimately, they are the ones who will guard the values of Passover and ensure that they continue to influence the world. As Rabbi Jonathan Sacks, the former Chief Rabbi of the United Kingdom, wrote: "The message of Passover remains as powerful as ever. Freedom is won not on the battlefield, but in the classroom and the home. Teach your children the history of freedom if you want them never to lose it."

Through asking questions, reading the Exodus story, and participating in a host of rituals throughout the night, we create an experience that remains deeply seared into our hearts and consciousness forever. The hope is that as we leave the *seder* table, we are different and better people than when we came to it. In this way, Passover night is present in our lives throughout the year and shapes future generations.

A well-known story is told about a *Seder* that was unlike any other, which captures the essence of what the *seder* experience is meant to be. The story goes that the holy sage, Rabbi Levi Yitzchak of Berditchev, had just finished conducting a master *Seder* for his disciples. As everyone was discussing how amazing the rabbi's *Seder* had been and how it was holier than any other, the rabbi heard a heavenly voice speaking to him: "Levi Yitzchak's *Seder* was pleasing to God, but there is a Jew in Berditchev called Shmerl the tailor whose *Seder* reached even higher!"

"Who is Shmerl the tailor?" the startled rabbi inquired of his students.

"Him? He's a drunkard who lives at the edge of town," replied the students.

"Please take me to him immediately," the rabbi requested.

When the great rabbi arrived at Shmerl's house, it was late at night. Shmerl's wife took one look at the saintly rabbi and went to get her husband saying, "The rabbi has come to punish you."

When Shmerl appeared, the rabbi said, "Please, tell me about your *Seder*."

At this, Shmerl began to wail and said, "Please Rebbe, don't punish me. It's not my fault…I didn't know any better…Please, have mercy"

The rabbi was astounded and wondered how this man's *Seder* could have been more holy than his. The rabbi reassured Shmerl, "I'm not here to reprimand you; I just want to know what you did at your *Seder*."

Shmerl eventually calmed down and explained, "I was so drunk that I fell asleep until my wife banged on my door and screamed that the children were getting tired and I needed to lead the *Seder*. I came out to my beautiful family and a *seder* table set to perfection. I felt so terrible and unworthy. The vodka was still swirling in my head. I looked at the table, turned to my family, and began to cry. I said, 'The truth is that I have no idea what I'm supposed to do with all of this stuff. I never had a chance to study and I can't even read the *haggadah*.' Looking at the innocent faces of my children I cried some more. Then I said: 'But dear, sweet children, I do know this one thing and you must know it, too! There is a God and He hears our prayers! A long time ago He sent a man named Moses to save the Jewish people and one day He will send the Messiah to save us, too!' Then I collapsed in my chair and fell asleep."

In the end, the *seder* night is not about going through the motions and getting through the lengthy *haggadah*. It's about having the *Seder* and the *haggadah* go through *us* and move *us*. It's about coming to deep realizations and evoking lasting transformations as we continue to write the next chapters in the Passover story that began three thousand years ago and which we relive on this sacred and powerful night.

THE PREPARATION

*A*traditional Jewish saying goes: "There can be no holiness without preparation." The perfect holiday doesn't just happen; it takes time and preparation, and this is especially true of Passover. The spirit of the holiday fills our minds and homes for days, weeks, and even months before Passover begins.

The primary reason for this preparation is the biblical directive to rid our homes of any leavened products: "*For seven days you are to eat bread made without yeast. On the first day remove the yeast from your houses* " (Exodus 12:15). This commandment expresses itself in what is often referred to as the Jewish version of spring cleaning. We search our homes for any trace of products containing yeast, known in Hebrew as *chametz*, and get rid of them.

Well before the holiday, we begin going through every part of our homes. We search behind and under furniture, we go through the pockets of our clothing, and generally clean out all parts of our homes where any food might have been left behind, like between the couch cushions or inside desk drawers. The house gets a thorough cleaning, and no stone goes unturned.

As the holiday draws closer, we prepare our kitchens. After being carefully cleaned, we cover kitchen countertops and any other surfaces used for food. We place stove grates through fire or in an oven, and set our ovens to the highest temperatures possible in order to burn off all remnants of food. Once everything is ready, we take out pots, pans, and dishes that have been designated specifically for Passover use. Our regular kitchenware is set aside, and some people even tape off cupboards containing non-Passover items so they will not be touched. The cabinets that we do use are often labeled "kosher for Passover."

The first ritual of Passover occurs the night before the observance begins. On the night of the fourteenth of *Nissan*, we engage in a ritual known as *bedikat chametz*, checking for *chametz*. Ten pieces of leavened bread are hidden throughout the home and then searched out. With the lights off, we search our homes in candlelight (or by flashlight). We find the ten hidden pieces and any other *chametz* that we may have forgotten and collect them in a bag. We recite a prayer that proclaims that we disown any remnants of *chametz* that we may not have found and declare that they are "like dust of the earth." The next day, we burn the ten pieces along with any other lingering *chametz* in a ceremony called *biur chametz*, or burning *chametz*. At this point, our preparation is complete.

Preparing for Passover and ridding our homes of *chametz* is a lengthy and tedious process. However, our actions are deeply symbolic and intended to influence our hearts. This idea is best expressed in an ancient prayer that many Jews recite as they search for *chametz*: "May it be Your will God that You enable us to explore and search out our spiritual maladies and return in complete repentance before You."

At the end of the process, our hearts as well as our homes are prepared for Passover.

THE *SEDER* TABLE

When guests arrive for a Passover *Seder*, the first thing they will notice is the *seder* table. A beautifully set table sets the tone for the evening. As such, we are careful to make sure that everything is set and ready to go before the holiday even begins.

The word "table" in Hebrew is *shulchan*, which is composed of the words *shel* and *chen*, meaning "a place of kindness" or "a place of grace." Our tables are far more than a functional element in our homes; they are a vehicle for bringing goodness and godliness into the world.

Traditionally, we use a white tablecloth for our *seder* tables. White symbolizes holiness and purity, the perfect backdrop for our holiday celebration. We light two candles, which represent both peace in the home and bringing light into the world. It is also customary to have flowers adorn the table in order to enhance its beauty. Before we even sit down, the table should take us into a sacred space and prepare us for a special night.

On Passover, our tables go beyond the traditional holiday table settings. The *seder* table is brimming with symbolic foods and objects that will be used throughout the evening. This is because on Passover, the holiday table takes on an additional role. Aside from being a place where we feed others and connect with God, it also becomes the place where we share our story. We speak and listen as we are nourished, both body and soul.

THE *SEDER* PLATE

To help us relive the Exodus on Passover, the *seder* table is adorned with a *seder* plate, *k'ara* in Hebrew, that contains six items. Each of these items helps us to see, taste, and feel the Exodus story; each is abounding with meaning and symbolism. Quite literally, they are food for thought on *seder* night. Below are the six elements found on every *seder* plate.

***Zeroah*, Roasted Bone** – A roasted animal bone represents the Passover offering that was brought first on the eve of the Exodus by the Israelites, and then, every year that the Temple stood in Jerusalem. While this sacrifice was originally a lamb, today we commonly use a poultry wing or neck. This symbol reminds us that God "passed over" the houses of the Israelites during the plague of the deaths of the firstborn. It also alludes to the faith of the Israelites as they prepared and brought that first Passover offering. Moreover, the *zeroah* calls our attention to a verse where God promises to redeem Israel with a *zeroah netuya*, an outstretched arm: *"I will free you from being slaves to them, and I will redeem you with an outstretched arm"* (Exodus 6:6).

***Beitza*, Egg** – The egg, which is boiled and then roasted, symbolizes a second offering that was brought during Temple times. Along with the Passover offering, Jews would bring a holiday sacrifice that was brought on all festivals mentioned in the Bible. An egg was chosen to represent this offering because in Judaism, an egg symbolizes mourning and is the traditional food of mourners. On Passover night, we remember that we still mourn the loss of the Holy Temple and that we yearn for our ultimate redemption, another theme of Passover.

***Maror*, Bitter Herbs** – The bitterness of slavery is a central theme on Passover. Traditionally, we use grated horseradish root to serve as our bitter herbs and bitter-tasting leafy greens as our bitter vegetable. Both recall the cruelty that the Israelites endured as slaves in Egypt. The horseradish is more sharp, the lettuce more bitter. On this night of celebration, both of these elements help us focus on the bitterness that once was.

***Haroset,* Paste** – *Haroset* is a mixture made of fruit, nuts, and wine, which are chopped finely or blended into a paste-like consistency. The *haroset* is meant to look like the mortar that the Israelites were forced to use as slaves to create the bricks used to build Egyptian cities. However, the *haroset* tastes sweet, reminding us that even in bitter times, we can always find something sweet in our lives and that bitter times are eventually followed by the sweetness of salvation.

***Karpas,* Vegetable** – Any vegetable can be used for this symbol, but it is customary to choose something green such as parsley, celery, or a cucumber, because this *seder* symbol reminds us that God took the Israelites out of Egypt during the spring. It is a symbol of redemption.

***Hazeret,* Bitter Vegetable** – Like the bitter herbs, the bitter vegetable, usually romaine lettuce or endives, symbolize the harshness of Egyptian slavery.

The *seder* plate

MATZAH

At Passover, *matzah* is by far the most symbolic and deeply meaningful element on the table. Eating *matzah* during Passover is a direct commandment from the Bible: *"...for seven days eat unleavened bread, the bread of affliction, because you left Egypt in haste—so that all the days of your life you may remember the time of your departure from Egypt"* (Deuteronomy 16:3). It is the *matzah* that most captures the Exodus story, and it is through the *matzah* that we can best relive the story on *seder* night.

Every *seder* table must contain at least three whole *matzot*. Alternatively, the *matzot* are placed on a large plate and separated by cloth or napkins and covered on top. During the *Seder*, they are "'unveiled" at specific times in the story. While these three *matzot* play an integral role in telling the Exodus story, most people have plenty of *matzah* available and placed on the table for everyone to eat throughout the night.

The sages suggest a few reasons for why specifically three *matzot* are needed for the *Seder*. Some explain that they represent the three Patriarchs – Abraham, Isaac, and Jacob – in whose merit the redemption occurred. Others teach that the three *matzot* represent the three groups of the population who were redeemed – the priests, the Levites, and the children of Israel. However, symbolism aside, the three *matzot* serve a practical purpose. Toward the beginning of the *Seder*, the middle *matzah* is broken. Later on we will make the ceremonial blessing on the *matzah* "bread" and two whole *matzot* are required, the same way that two loaves of bread are required on all other holidays and on the Sabbath. Together, all three *matzot* are necessary in order for our *Seder* to be complete.

The flat cracker-like bread has a few names besides *matzah*, and each name speaks to a different part of its symbolism. Scripture refers to *matzah* as *"the bread of affliction"* and it is also dubbed "the poor man's bread" as only two ingredients are needed to make *matzah* — water and flour. No sugar, no oil, and certainly, no yeast. *Matzah* contains only the bare essentials, signifying a life of poverty and difficulty. It recalls the harsh slavery in Egypt.

However, *matzah* is also referred to as "the bread of freedom." *Matzah* is introduced in the Exodus narrative when the children of Israel were forced to leave Egypt in such a hurry that they didn't have time to allow their dough to rise. *Matzah* reminds us of leaving Egypt, and therefore, is a symbol of our freedom.

Finally, *matzah* is also called "the food of faith." This title links the other two names and also encapsulates the message of the *Seder*. It takes faith to see our afflictions as precursors to redemption. The *matzah* is the link between slavery and freedom, reminding us that God hears our prayers and brings about redemption.

Passover bread with garlic

THE FOUR CUPS OF WINE

O n *seder* night, everyone is considered royalty. As we celebrate our freedom and our special relationship with our God, the King of kings, we demonstrate that we are privileged people. One way that we do this is by drinking four cups of wine (or grape juice) at specific points in the *Seder* — at the opening, after we tell the Exodus story, after we eat the festive meal, and after we sing praises to God. Wine is considered a luxury; it is a royal drink that celebrates our freedom and is a key symbol at our *seder* table.

As the table is set for *seder* night, each guest is given a wine glass. In accordance with the theme of royalty, no one pours his or her own wine. Rather, each participant has his or her glass filled by another guest, emphasizing that we are nobility on this night. Additionally, it is customary to lean to the left while drinking the wine. Royals of the past were known to recline on couches as they drank their wine, and this is

the atmosphere that we seek to create. Many homes place pillows or cushions on every chair in order to make the drinking and reclining experience even more comfortable and authentic.

The prevailing custom is to serve only red wines at the *Seder*. The color red is symbolic of the blood of the Passover lamb. The blood of the lamb represents liberation since it was used to mark the children of Israel's homes on the eve of the Exodus, both saving them from the plague of the death of the firstborn and also making them worthy of God's salvation. The red wine reminds us of faith and redemption.

The drinking of wine is a focal point of the night, but why four cups of wine? On the Sabbath and other festivals, we begin our meals by sanctifying the day over one cup of wine. Why don't we do the same on Passover?

The sages explain that the four cups of wine correspond to the four expressions that God used when describing how He would save the children of Israel: *"I am the LORD, and I will bring you out from under the yoke of the Egyptians. I will free you from being slaves to them, and I will redeem you with an outstretched arm and with mighty acts of judgment. I will take you as my own people, and I will be your God"* (Exodus 6:6–7). As we drink the four cups of wine, we remember God's four promises: *"I will bring you out," "I will free you," "I will redeem you,"* and *"I will take you."*

These four expressions of salvation correspond to four stages in the redemption process. As we go through the *Seder* and recreate the Exodus experience, we celebrate each stage of our salvation and appreciate the process through which God set us free.

THE CUP OF ELIJAH

As was explained in the previous section, we drink four cups of wine during the *Seder*, which correspond to God's four promises of salvation. However, the truth is that God makes a fifth promise.

Matzah *and goblet*

After God promised *"I will bring you out,"* *"I will free you,"* *"I will redeem you,"* and *"I will take you"* (Exodus 6:6–7), He says: *"And I will bring you to the land I swore with uplifted hand to give to Abraham, to Isaac and to Jacob. I will give it to you as a possession"* (Exodus 6:8). *"I will bring you"* is the fifth promise of salvation, and accordingly, there is also a fifth cup of wine.

However, this fifth cup is separate and different from the first four. This is because the fifth promise differs from the other four. The first four promises all have to do with the Exodus story in which the Israelites were taken out of Egypt, culminating with the giving of the *Torah* at Mount Sinai. The fifth promise refers to the storyline that begins in the book of Joshua, when God brought the Israelites to the Promised Land and they inherited it.

Additionally, the fifth cup is set aside from the other four because, on a symbolic level, the full redemption of the children of Israel is not yet complete. While long ago, God brought the Jewish people out of Egypt, we have still not fully realized the promise of coming to the land of Israel in order to fully possess it for all of eternity. According to Jewish tradition, only the coming of the Messiah will bring this promise to fruition.

The fifth cup, which is often larger and more ornate than the others, is placed on the table at the beginning of the *Seder*, but is only filled toward the end. After we conclude the Grace After Meals and drink the third cup of wine, we fill the fifth cup – but we do not drink it. It is reserved for the spirit of the prophet Elijah, whom we welcome to the *Seder* by opening the front door at this time.

In Jewish tradition, Elijah is the harbinger of the Messiah. As we read in Scripture: *"See, I will send the prophet Elijah to you before that great and dreadful day of the Lord comes"* (Malachi 4:5). Since the fifth cup represents the ultimate redemption, it has become known as the Cup of Elijah, who will herald our redemption. Accordingly, the *seder* night is not only for remembering our salvation in the past; it is also meant to prepare us for our future redemption. As we open the door for Elijah and pour a cup of wine for him, we express our yearning for the messianic age to begin.

THE SEDER

INTRODUCTION

*T*he *Seder* is the heart of the Passover celebration. It is through the *Seder* that we fulfill the biblical injunction to *"tell your children and grandchildren how I dealt harshly with the Egyptians and how I performed my signs among them"* (Exodus 10:2). The *haggadah*, which means "the telling," is the book that serves as our guide for the night. It is a step-by-step guide that contains all the rituals, texts, and prayers that are said throughout the evening.

photo credit-mikhail-Shutterstock.com

The *Seder* is usually run by a "leader," who can be a community leader, the senior family member, or anyone who is capable of doing so. The leader helps move the *Seder* along and keeps everyone on track while reciting certain key passages. However, it is important to remember

that participation is encouraged from all *seder* participants, and it is highly recommended that the readings in the *haggadah* be divided and shared. Asking questions is also a key component to a successful *Seder*, as is adding our own personal insights, reflections, and stories. We are encouraged to be creative, stay curious, and above all, be involved. In the words of the *haggadah*, "Every person must see himself or herself as personally having left Egypt."

ON THE *SEDER* TABLE

At the start of the *Seder*, a number of items need to be on the table. The most central element on the table is the *seder* plate containing a roasted bone, roasted egg, *karpas* vegetable, bitter vegetables, bitter herbs, and the *haroset* mixture. Some *seder* plates come with a compartment underneath for placing the three ritual *matzot*; however, a plate with the three *matzot* placed near the leader is also sufficient. In either case, it is customary to cover the *matzot* with a special cloth or napkin until they are used.

Also on the table are the Cup of Elijah and the other items that are used throughout the evening. Depending on the size of the *Seder*, one of each of these items will suffice, or sometimes, the host will place a few of each item along the table. These items include: a bowl of saltwater; a bowl of *haroset*; a plate containing a stack of *matzah* (also covered); a dish with small pieces of the *karpas* vegetable; and a plate filled with the bitter vegetables.

In addition, every place setting must contain a wine glass and wine or grape juice should already be on the table. It is ideal to provide every participant with a *haggadah* so that each person can follow along and participate. Pillow cushions, to enhance the feeling of freedom and nobility, are optional.

THE FIFTEEN STEPS

Seder literally means "order," and the Passover *Seder* is a deliberately designed experience containing fifteen steps placed in sequential order. These fifteen steps correspond to the fifteen literal steps that led to the Holy Temple in Jerusalem and the fifteen psalms that King David penned, called the *Songs of Ascent*, which were intended to be sung on each step. Just as the steps in the Temple and the psalms were intended to bring a person closer to God, the *seder* experience is intended to raise a person up and out of bondage and closer to the freedom experienced in serving the Lord.

The fifteen steps are read aloud at the start of the *Seder* to provide a roadmap for the evening. When followed correctly, they will lead us from the depths of slavery to the experience of redemption as we fulfill the biblical obligation to retell and relive the Exodus story.

THE FIFTEEN STEPS:

Kadesh, **sanctifying the day** — We recite the *Kiddush,* the blessing over wine, which sanctifies this night.

Urchatz, **ritual hand washing** — We physically and symbolically wash our hands.

Karpas, **eating the karpas vegetable** — We eat a vegetable dipped in salt water.

Yachatz, **breaking the middle matzah** — We break the middle *matzah* and set aside the larger half.

Maggid, **telling the story** — We tell the story of the Exodus by reading the *haggadah.*

Rachtzah, **hand washing with a blessing** — We wash our hands in preparation for eating *matzah.*

Motzi, **blessing before eating bread** — We recite the traditional blessing before eating bread.

Matzah, **blessing and eating the matzah** – We fulfill the biblical obligation to eat *matzah.*

Maror, **eating the bitter herbs** — We eat bitter herbs dipped in the *haroset* mixture.

Korech, **Hillel's sandwich** – We eat a combination of *matzah,* bitter herbs, and *haroset.*

Shulchan Orech, **eating the meal** – We celebrate with a festive meal befitting the holiday.

Tzafun, **eating the afikomen** – We eat the larger portion of the *matzah* broken earlier.

Barech, **blessing after eating** – We recite the traditional Grace After Meals.

Hallel, **songs of praise** – We recite psalms of thanksgiving and faith.

Nirtzah, **conclusion of the Seder** – We conclude the *Seder* with songs and prayers.

Temple steps in Jerusalem which correspond to the fifteen Songs of Ascent in the Psalms

1. KADESH —
SANCTIFYING THE DAY

The first cup is filled with either wine or grape juice.

As a sign that we are like royalty on this night, it is customary that no participant fills his or her own glass. Rather, we fill each other's cups. Participants then rise as the leader recites the Kiddush, *the blessings that sanctify the night, while holding the cup of wine. Once the leader has concluded the blessing, all participants are seated and drink from their cups. Traditionally, we recline toward the left while drinking, another sign of nobility and freedom.*

LEADER: Blessed are You, LORD, our God, King of the universe, who creates the fruit of the vine.

ALL: Amen

LEADER: Blessed are You, LORD, our God, King of the universe, who has chosen us from among all people, and raised us above all tongues, and made us holy through His commandments. And You have given us, LORD, our God, in love, festivals for happiness, feasts and festive seasons for rejoicing the day of this Feast of *Matzot* and this Festival of holy convocation, the Season of our Freedom, a holy convocation, commemorating the departure from Egypt. For You have chosen us and sanctified us from all the nations, and You have given us as a heritage Your holy Festivals, in happiness and joy. Blessed are You, God, who sanctifies Israel and the festive seasons.

ALL: Amen

LEADER: Blessed are You, LORD, our God, King of the universe, who has kept us alive and sustained us and brought us to this festive season.

ALL: Amen

COMMENTARY ON KADESH

In the Jewish tradition, every Sabbath and festival meal begins with the Kiddush, *the blessing over wine that designates the day as* kadosh, *Hebrew for holy. We drink wine to set apart this time as holy because wine is among the most valued drinks in the world and lends importance to this day. Additionally, wine goes through a lengthy and meticulous process in order to achieve its value. Similarly and symbolically, holiness and the refinement of our souls are only attained through hard work over a long period of time. As we designate our holidays as holy days, we remember that holiness comes through service, and we prepare for worship.*

COMMENTARY ON URCHATZ

Usually, ritual hand washing is done right before eating bread or matzah, unleavened bread. However, on this night, we engage in the hand washing early on, long before we partake of any matzah. One reason we do this is because this hand washing is not about the physical food we are going to partake; it is connected to the "soul food" that we are about to receive. As we wash our hands, we prepare ourselves for a sacred experience and designate all our actions, as symbolized by our hands, for holy purposes.

2. URCHATZ —
RITUAL HAND WASHING

The leader (or in some traditions, all participants) engages in ritual hand washing. We pour water from a cup, first twice on the right hand and then twice on the left. It is customary to have a cup filled with water, a basin, and a towel brought to the table (instead of participants going to a kitchen or bathroom to wash hands) as yet another sign of freedom and dignity. No blessing is said, and we proceed immediately to the next step.

3. *KARPAS* —
EATING THE KARPAS VEGETABLE

Any vegetable can be used as karpas but it is customary to use a green vegetable such as parsley, celery, or cucumber. Each participant takes a small piece of the vegetable, dips it in saltwater, recites the blessing, and then eats the vegetable.

ALL: Blessed are You, LORD, our God, King of the universe, who creates the fruit of the earth.

Table ready for traditional seder *ritual during the Jewish holiday of Passover*

> ### COMMENTARY ON *KARPAS*
>
> *We have not yet begun our festive meal, nor have we begun in earnest to tell the Exodus story, so why are we dipping vegetables in saltwater at this point? One reason is to arouse the curiosity of the children at the table — and the inner child of each adult. As we begin the* Seder, *we remember that an important theme of the night is to ask questions, to seek understanding, and to encourage others to do the same. In order for the* Seder *to be an impactful learning experience, there has to be a desire to learn. We do things out of the ordinary so as to spark that passion for learning.*
>
> *The lesson here comes from the symbolism of eating the vegetable and saltwater together. The vegetable symbolizes spring, which is when God redeemed the children of Israel. Spring also reminds us of renewal and new life. In contrast, the saltwater recalls the sweat and tears the Israelites shed in slavery under Egyptian oppression. On Passover, we bring bondage and redemption together as a reminder that both difficulties and miracles are part of the salvation process.*

COMMENTARY ON *YACHATZ*

Matzah *is also known as* lechem oni *in Hebrew, which means "poor man's bread," as it contains nothing more than flour and water. It is also referred to as* lechem she-onim alav, *a Hebrew play on words that means "bread that we speak about." Matzah is the symbol that begins the story. We break the middle piece in half because poor people are often forced to divide their meals, putting away the rest so that they will have something to eat later. We keep the smaller piece of* matzah *on the table. It brings us to the starting point of the Exodus story. We envision ourselves as poor and oppressed people who don't know where our next meal is coming from or what the future will hold. The broken* matzah *is a symbol of our brokenness and the brokenness of the world. Now we will begin the journey toward wholeness.*

4. *YACHATZ—* BREAKING THE MIDDLE *MATZAH*

The leader breaks the middle of the three matzot *into two pieces. The larger half is wrapped in a napkin and set aside for the end of the meal. The smaller half is returned to its place between the other two* matzot *and serves as the springboard for the next step where we will begin to tell the Exodus story.*

Breaking the matzah *bread*

5. MAGGID—
TELLING THE STORY

*T*his section forms the bulk of the Seder. Maggid *mean "to tell," and it is this step of the* Seder *from which the* haggadah *gets its name. During this portion of the* Seder, *we do the actual telling of the Passover story. Why is a lengthy discussion about the Exodus story such a critical part of celebrating Passover? The answer is because the ability to speak is what most distinguishes humans from every other form of creation. Our capability to express ourselves is a direct result of our ability to think, understand, come to conclusions, and make plans. Speech gives us the power to create. It bridges our thoughts with our actions. When God created the world, He "spoke" it into being. On* seder *night, we use our God-given gift of speech in order to build a better world. Together, we share stories of the past and inspire a better future.*

THE BREAD OF AFFLICTION

The matzot *are uncovered and the plate is lifted up for all to see. The telling of the Exodus story begins with the following words.*

ALL: This is the bread of affliction that our fathers ate in the land of Egypt. Whoever is hungry, let him come and eat; whoever is in need, let him come and conduct the *Seder* of Passover. This year we are here; next year in the land of Israel. This year we are slaves; next year we will be free people.

The matzot *are put down and covered.*

COMMENTARY ON "THE BREAD OF AFFLICTION"

It seems fitting enough that we begin telling the Exodus story by recalling the matzah *that symbolizes our affliction. However, why do we also start by inviting the hungry to eat with us? Surely, invitations would have been more effective before our* Seder *has begun! There are two explanations. First, as we tell the story of our redemption, we take time to remember those who are less fortunate than we are. Even in our greatest joy, we must always remember that our joy cannot be complete if other people are still living in pain; it is our job to help those in need as best as we can. Second, we understand that this invitation is for us as well, as people who are hungry for God's Word and who are in need of God's intervention. We invite ourselves to really be present at the* Seder. *All who sincerely hunger for God will be satisfied on this night.*

THE FOUR QUESTIONS

The second cup of wine (grape juice) is filled.

It is customary for the youngest child present to recite The Four Questions. If no child is present, then any adult may do so.

READER: Why is this night different from all other nights?

On all other nights we do not dip even once; on this night we dip twice!

On all other nights we eat *chametz* (leavened bread) or *matzah* (unleavened bread); on this night only *matzah*!

On all other nights we eat all kinds of vegetables; on this night we eat bitter vegetables!

On all other nights we eat sitting upright or reclining; on this night we all recline!

COMMENTARY ON "THE FOUR QUESTIONS"

As the storytelling gets underway, we begin with questions. The reason we start this way, as opposed to simply telling the story, is because of the biblical verse that says: "In days to come, when your son asks you, 'What does this mean?' say to him, 'With a mighty hand the LORD brought us out of Egypt'" *(Exodus 13:14). The Bible specifies that our children should ask first, and then we should answer. The sages explain that this question-and-answer format is the most powerful way to teach and share our story. Someone who thinks that he or she knows everything will have a hard time learning anything new. But when we ask questions, we create a space for answers – answers that will reach deep inside us and remain with us long after the* Seder *has concluded.*

Children are the ideal questioners, and when they are present, they are the focus during much of the Seder. *Judaism recognizes that the future lies in our children and that building a better tomorrow begins with them. On Passover, we share our heritage with our children, in the hope that they will carry on our legacy.*

WE WERE SLAVES

The matzot *are uncovered as we answer the questioner with the following:*

LEADER: We were slaves to Pharaoh in Egypt, and the LORD, our God, took us out from there with a strong hand and with an outstretched arm. If the Holy One, blessed be He, had not taken our fathers out of Egypt, then we, our children and our children's children would have remained enslaved to Pharaoh in Egypt. Even if all of us were wise, all of us understanding, all of us knowing the *Torah*, we would still be obligated to discuss the Exodus from Egypt; and everyone who discusses the Exodus from Egypt at length is praiseworthy.

COMMENTARY ON "WE WERE SLAVES"

The first line of this paragraph provides the key to the Seder. *The reason for our* Seder *is the commemoration of both the enslavement of the children of Israel and God's salvation. The text concludes by reminding us of the importance of discussing the Exodus story. In the middle of the paragraph we find the seemingly strange statement that if God hadn't freed the Israelites, then we would all still be enslaved. But is that really true? Surely someone would have come along in the last few thousand years to free us.*

The sages explain that there is a difference between man-made salvation and godly salvation. A human could have only freed us physically, but God freed us physically and spiritually. If God hadn't freed us, then we would still be slaves – maybe not to Pharaoh himself, but to his self-indulgent and self-defeating mentality.

A Controversy Whatsoever on Talmud, *by Carl Schleicher (1859 – after 1871),*
19th century , oil on panel, 25.5 × 31 cm (10 × 12.2 in)

THE WISE MEN

READER: It once happened that Rabbi Eliezer, Rabbi Yehoshua, Rabbi Elazar the son of Azariah, Rabbi Akiva, and Rabbi Tarfon were celebrating the *Seder* in B'nei Brak. They were discussing the Exodus from Egypt the entire night, until their students came and told them: "Our teachers! The time has come for reciting the morning *Shema*!"

Rabbi Eleazar the son of Azariah said, "I am like a man of seventy years old, yet I was never able to convince my colleagues that one is obligated to mention the Exodus from Egypt at night, until Ben Zoma explained it: It is stated in the *Torah*, *'that all the days of your life you may remember the time of your departure from Egypt'* (Deuteronomy 16:3). *'The days of your life'* refers only to the days; *'all the days of your life'* on the other hand, includes the nights, too."

The sages say: *"The days of your life"* indicates this life, but *"all the days of your life"* includes the messianic times as well.

COMMENTARY ON "THE WISE MEN"

In the previous section, we just finished saying that even if we were all wise and fully aware of the Exodus story, we still would be obligated to discuss it on Passover because the obligation to do so is not so much about knowing the story as much as feeling and experiencing the story. Now the haggadah *provides us with a case in point. These wise men were obviously very familiar with the Exodus story, and yet they talked about it so much at their* Seder *that their students had to notify them that the time for the next morning's prayers had come. The remaining part of the reading explains that remembering the Exodus story is so important that we must actively do so day and night, both in the present and in the messianic times to come.*

THE FOUR SONS

ALL: Blessed is the Omnipresent One, blessed be He! Blessed is He who gave the *Torah* to His people Israel, blessed be He!

READER: The *Torah* speaks of four children: One is wise, one is wicked, one is simple, and one does not know how to ask.

What does the wise son say? "What are *'these are the commands, decrees and laws the LORD your God directed me to teach you'* (Deuteronomy 6:1)? You, in turn, will instruct him in the laws of Passover, up to "one is not to eat any dessert after the Passover lamb."

What does the wicked son say? *"What does this ceremony mean to you?"* (Exodus 12:26). He says "to you," but not to him! Therefore, because he has excluded himself from the community, he has denied the foundation of our faith; consequently, you must blunt his teeth and say to him: *"I do this because of what the LORD did for me when I came out of Egypt"* (Exodus 13:8); "for me" — but not for him! If he had been there, he would not have been redeemed!

What does the simple son say? *"What does this mean?"* (Exodus 13:14). You will say to him: *"With a mighty hand the LORD brought us out of Egypt, out of the land of slavery"* (Exodus 13:14).

As for the son who does not know how to ask, you must begin to speak with him, as it is said: *"On that day tell your son, 'I do this because of what the LORD did for me when I came out of Egypt'"* (Exodus 13:8).

COMMENTARY ON "THE FOUR SONS"

So far in this storytelling part of the Seder, *we have asked some fundamental questions, given some basic answers, and spoken about the importance of discussing the Exodus story in a deep and meaningful way. Now we turn to the "Four Sons" who represent four types of learners. As we continue to teach and learn about the Exodus story, we recognize that different people learn in different ways. For the wise son who is capable of understanding all the Passover laws, we teach him everything thoroughly. The wicked son gets a dose of tough love, and the simple son receives answers that he is capable of comprehending. For the son who doesn't even know or care enough to ask questions, we reach out and initiate the conversation in a way that draws him in. We believe that no child – or adult – should be left behind. Everyone has a seat at the* seder *table and it is our job to make the service meaningful for all people.*

TIME OF THE TELLING

READER: One may think that the discussion of the Exodus must begin on the first day of the month of *Nissan*. Therefore, the *Torah* specifies: *"On that day"* (Exodus 13:8). The expression *"on that day,"* however, could mean that we need to speak about the Exodus while it is still daytime; therefore, the *Torah* adds that the father should say, *"I do this because…"* (Exodus 13:8). The expression *"I do this because…"* can only be said at a time when *matzah* and *maror* are placed before you.

COMMENTARY ON "TIME OF THE TELLING"

Now that we have discussed how to share the Exodus story, we are talking about when to tell it. This passage tells us that although we may have thought the first of the month is the appropriate time to begin talking about the Exodus, the correct time is really at the Seder *itself when the* matzah *and* maror *are in front of us. Why would we consider telling the Exodus story on the first of the Hebrew month of* Nissan *when Passover is on the fifteenth day of* Nissan? *The reason is because it was on the first of the month of* Nissan *that God gave the instructions regarding the Passover lamb.*

Next, the text considers that we may have thought that the fourteenth day of Nissan *would be the time to begin the discussion because it was on that day that the Israelites slaughtered the lamb. However, the text concludes that it is specifically on the night that the children of Israel were freed from Egypt that we are to tell the story. This is because at that exact time every year, in the Jewish tradition, there is the greatest potential for freedom and liberation from all our constraints – both physical and spiritual.*

IN THE BEGINNING

READER: In the beginning, our fathers served idols; but now the Omnipresent One has brought us to His service, as it is said: *"Joshua said to all the people, 'This is what the LORD, the God of Israel, says: "Long ago your ancestors, including Terah the father of Abraham and Nahor, lived beyond the Euphrates River and worshiped other gods. But I took your father Abraham from the land beyond the Euphrates and led him throughout Canaan and gave him many descendants. I gave him Isaac, and to Isaac I gave Jacob and Esau. I assigned the hill country of Seir to Esau, but Jacob and his family went down to Egypt"'"* (Joshua 24:2–4).

Blessed is He who keeps His promise to Israel, blessed be He! For the Holy One, blessed be He, calculated the end of the bondage, in order to do as He had said to our father Abraham at the "Covenant between the Portions," as it is said: *"Then the LORD said to him [Abraham], 'Know for certain that for four hundred years your descendants will be strangers in a country not their own and that they will be enslaved and mistreated there. But I will punish the nation they serve as slaves, and afterward they will come out with great possessions'"* (Genesis 15:13–14).

COMMENTARY ON "IN THE BEGINNING"

Now we begin to tell the Exodus story in an elaborated form. But where does the story start? With the children of Israel in Egypt? According to the haggadah, *the story begins long before the children of Israel were enslaved. This is the story of how Israel became a nation. It ends with the Exodus from Egypt and the giving of the* Torah *on Mount Sinai, but it begins with Abraham, or rather Abraham's father, Terah, who was an idol-worshiper. In this part of the storytelling, we zoom out and look at the larger picture that gives a more meaningful context for the Exodus. Our roots are in idolatry, but through a process that began with Abraham and ended with the Exodus, we were transformed – we were brought close to the one true God and to His service.*

GOD'S PROMISE

The matzot *are covered and our wine glasses are raised as we proclaim:*

ALL: This is what has stood by our fathers and us! For not only has one risen against us to destroy us, but in every generation they rise against us to destroy us; and the Holy One, blessed be He, saves us from their hands.

The wine glasses are set down and the matzot *are covered once more.*

COMMENTARY ON "GOD'S PROMISE"

We depart from the Exodus story for a moment in order to reflect upon how the story of Egyptian oppression is a story that has repeated itself throughout Jewish history, even today. In every generation, someone, somewhere, seeks to destroy the Jews. However, God faithfully saves the Jews every single time. In 1897, Mark Twain observed, "All things are mortal but the Jews.... What is the secret of his immortality?" In this text we answer, "This is what has stood by our fathers and us" – a reference to God's promise to Abraham in the covenant mentioned in the previous section. It is only because of God's promise to preserve the Jews that we are still here today.

THE STORY

We tell the Exodus story using Deuteronomy 26:5–8 as a framework, expounding upon every phrase. As the text is lengthy, it is advisable to divide the readings among the participants and encourage involvement.

READER: Go forth and learn what Laban the Aramean wanted to do to our father Jacob. Pharaoh had issued a decree against the male children only, but Laban wanted to uproot everyone — as it is said: *"My father was a wandering Aramean, and he went down into Egypt with a few people and lived there and became a great nation, powerful and numerous"* (Deuteronomy: 26:5).

"And he went down into Egypt" – forced by Divine decree.

"And lived there" – this teaches that our father Jacob did not go down to Egypt to settle, but only to live there temporarily. As it is said: *"They also said to him [Pharaoh], 'We have come to live here for a while, because the famine is severe in Canaan and your servants' flocks have no pasture. So now, please let your servants settle in Goshen'"* (Genesis 47:4).

"With a few people" – as it is said: *"Your ancestors who went down into Egypt were seventy in all, and now the LORD your God has made you as numerous as the stars in the sky"* (Deuteronomy 10:22).

"And became a great nation" – this teaches that Israel was distinctive there.

"Powerful" — as it is said: *"But the Israelites were exceedingly fruitful; they multiplied greatly, increased in numbers and became so numerous that the land was filled with them"* (Exodus 1:7).

"And numerous" – as it is said: *"Then I passed by and saw you kicking about in your blood, and as you lay there in your blood I said to you, 'Live!' I made you grow like a plant of the field. You grew and developed and entered puberty. Your breasts had formed and your hair had grown, yet you were stark naked"* (Ezekiel 16:6–7).

"But the Egyptians mistreated us and made us suffer, subjecting us to harsh labor" (Deuteronomy 26:6).

"The Egyptians mistreated us" – as it is said: *"Come, we must deal shrewdly with them or they will become even more numerous and, if war breaks out, will join our enemies, fight against us and leave the country"* (Exodus 1:10).

52

"And made us suffer"— as it is said: *"So they put slave masters over them to oppress them with forced labor, and they built Pithom and Rameses as store cities for Pharaoh"* (Exodus 1:11).

"Subjecting us to harsh labor" – as it is said: *"So the Egyptians came to dread the Israelites and worked them ruthlessly"* (Exodus 1:12–13).

***

"Then we cried out to the Lord, *the God of our ancestors, and the* Lord *heard our voice and saw our misery, toil and oppression"* (Deuteronomy 26:7).

"Then we cried out to the Lord, *the God of our ancestors"* – as it is said: *"During that long period, the king of Egypt died. The Israelites groaned in their slavery and cried out, and their cry for help because of their slavery went up to God"* (Exodus 2:23).

"And the Lord *heard our voice"* — as it is said: *"God heard their groaning and he remembered his covenant with Abraham, with Isaac and with Jacob"* (Exodus 2:24).

"And saw our misery" — this refers to the separation of husband and wife, as it is said:

"So God looked on the Israelites and was concerned about them" (Exodus 2:25).

"Toil" — this refers to the children, as it is said: *"Every Hebrew boy that is born you must throw into the Nile, but let every girl live"* (Exodus 1:22).

"Oppression" – this refers to the pressure, as it is said: *"And now the cry of the Israelites has reached me, and I have seen the way the Egyptians are oppressing them"* (Exodus 3:9).

***

"So the Lord *brought us out of Egypt with a mighty hand and an outstretched arm, with great terror and with signs and wonders"* (Deuteronomy 26:8).

"The Lord *brought us out of Egypt"* – not through an angel, not through a seraph and not through a messenger. The Holy One, blessed be He, did it in His glory by Himself! As it is said: *"On that same night I will pass through Egypt and strike down every firstborn of both people and animals, and I will bring judgment on all the gods of Egypt. I am the* Lord*"* (Exodus 12:12).

"I will pass through Egypt" – I, and not an angel;

"And strike down every firstborn of both people and animals" – I, and not a seraph;

"And I will bring judgment on all the gods of Egypt" – I, and not a messenger;

"I am the Lord" – it is I, and none other!

"With a mighty hand" – this refers to the pestilence as it is said: *"The hand of the Lord will bring a terrible plague on your livestock in the field — on your horses, donkeys and camels and on your cattle, sheep and goats"* (Exodus 9:3).

"And an outstretched arm" – this refers to the sword, as it is said: *"David looked up and saw the angel of the Lord standing between heaven and earth, with a drawn sword in his hand extended over Jerusalem"* (1 Chronicles 21:16).

"With great terror" – this refers to the revelation of the Divine Presence, as it is said: *"Has any god ever tried to take for himself one nation out of another nation, by testings, by signs and wonders, by war, by a mighty hand and an outstretched arm, or by great and awesome deeds, like all the things the Lord your God did for you in Egypt before your very eyes?"* (Deuteronomy 4:34).

"And with signs" – this refers to the staff, as it is said: *"But take this staff in your hand so you can perform the signs with it"* (Exodus 4:17).

"And wonders" – this refers to the blood, as it is said: *"I will show wonders in the heavens and on the earth"* (Joel 2:30).

Using our finger, we remove a drop of wine from our glasses as we say each of the following three terms:

ALL: *"Blood and fire and billows of smoke"* (Joel 2:30).

COMMENTARY ON "THE STORY"

The four verses from Deuteronomy provide a neat and concise basis for telling the Exodus story. The first verse tells us how the children of Israel ended up in Egypt in the first place — it was meant to be a temporary stay due to famine, but ended up becoming a new home where Jacob's progeny flourished. The next verse explains that the Israelites were ultimately oppressed and enslaved. The following verse tells us that the Israelites called out to God, and the final verse declares that God heard their prayers, intervened, and saved them with great miracles.

Together, these verses not only tell the Exodus story but also highlight the major themes of Passover as well as the foundations of our faith: that God controls history, that He cares about humanity and hears our prayers, and that He intervenes in order to bring about salvation.

We end this section with the introduction of the plagues that God inflicted on Egypt, and we will continue to speak about them in the sections that follow. In each instance, we pour out some wine from our cups as we mention the plagues as a sign that our joy is decreased. The sages teach that when the wicked Egyptians were drowning in the Red Sea, the angels wanted to sing praises to God. God responded: "The creations of My hands are drowning in the sea, and you are singing songs?" While we rejoice at God's justice, we take no pleasure in human suffering. We remove some wine, a symbol of our joy, as a sign of respect and sensitivity to all of God's creations.

THE TEN PLAGUES

We continue our explanation of Deuteronomy 26:8, which contains a reference to the ten plagues. As we say each of the plagues and then the three acronyms for the plagues, we use a finger to remove a drop of wine from our cups.

READER: Another explanation: "mighty hand" indicates two plagues; "outstretched arm," another two; "great terror," another two; "signs," another two; and "wonders," another two.

    These are the ten plagues which the Holy One, blessed be He, brought upon the Egyptians, namely as follows:

ALL: Blood
Frogs
Lice
Wild Beasts
Pestilence
Boils
Hail
Locust
Darkness
Slaying of the Firstborn

READER: Rabbi Yehudah referred to them by acronyms:

ALL: *DeTzaCh* (blood, frogs, lice)
ADaSh (beasts, pestilence, boils)
BeAChaV (hail, locust, darkness, firstborn)

COMMENTARY ON "THE TEN PLAGUES"

Why did Rabbi Yehudah find it necessary to create acronyms for the ten plagues, and moreover, why does the haggadah *contain them? The sages explain that these acronyms provide an easier way to remember the ten plagues in the right order – they also teach us something about the nature of the plagues. Each group demonstrated one of three fundamental principles of our faith. The first group of plagues established that God exists. The second group demonstrated God's providence and His mastery over the land. The third set revealed the truth of prophecy and established the validity of God's prophets. The goal of the plagues was not just to smite the Egyptians; it was also to teach the world that God exists and is involved in our lives.*

COUNTING THE PLAGUES

READER: Rabbi Yose the Galilean said:

How do you know that the Egyptians were stricken by ten plagues in Egypt, and then were struck by fifty plagues at the sea?

Of the plagues in Egypt, it says, *"The magicians said to Pharaoh, 'This is the finger of God'"* (Exodus 8:19). Of those by the sea, however, it says, *"And when the Israelites saw the mighty hand of the LORD displayed against the Egyptians, the people feared the LORD and put their trust in him and in Moses his servant"* (Exodus 14:31).

Now, how many plagues did they receive with *"the finger"*? Ten plagues!

Then it follows that since there were ten plagues in Egypt, there were fifty at the sea.

Rabbi Eliezer said:

How do we know that each individual plague which the Holy One, blessed be He, brought upon the Egyptians in Egypt consisted of four plagues?

For it is stated: *"He unleashed against them his hot anger, his wrath, indignation and hostility—a band of destroying angels"* (Psalm 78:49): *"wrath"* is one; *"indignation"* makes two; *"hostility"* makes three; *"a band of destroying angels"* makes four.

Consequently, they were struck by forty plagues in Egypt, and two hundred plagues at the sea.

Rabbi Akiva said:

How do we know that each individual plague which the Holy One, blessed be He, brought upon the Egyptians in Egypt consisted of five plagues?

For it is stated *"He unleashed against them his hot anger, his wrath, indignation and hostility—a band of destroying angels"* (Psalm 78:49): *"His hot anger"* is one; *"wrath"* makes two; *"indignation"* makes three; *"hostility"* makes four; *"a band of destroying angels"* makes five.

Consequently, they were struck by fifty plagues in Egypt, and 250 plagues at the sea.

COMMENTARY ON "COUNTING THE PLAGUES"

In this section, the sages go to great lengths to prove the multitude of plagues that God placed on the Egyptians. The basic premise is that if God used His "finger" in Egypt and His "hand" (all five fingers) at sea, then however many plagues occurred in Egypt should be multiplied by five to reach the number of plagues at the sea. The sages were invested in discovering the true amount of plagues that were inflicted on Egypt because they wanted to reveal the full range of miracles that God performed on behalf of the children of Israel. The more we see God's miracles, the greater our gratitude will be, and the more we will praise Him.

DAYENU!

The hymn Dayenu *is usually sung together by all of the participants; however, it can also be read by a reader with the participants joining in for the recurring word* Dayenu, *which means "It would have sufficed for us."*

READER: How many levels of favors has the Omnipresent One bestowed upon us?

READER or **ALL:** If He had brought us out from Egypt, but not carried out judgments against them —
Dayenu, it would have sufficed for us!

If He had carried out judgments against them, but not against their idols —
Dayenu, it would have sufficed for us!

If He had destroyed their idols, but not smitten their firstborn —
Dayenu, it would have sufficed for us!

If He had smitten their firstborn, but not given us their wealth —
Dayenu, it would have sufficed for us!

If He had given us their wealth, but not split the sea for us —
Dayenu, it would have sufficed for us!

If He had split the sea for us, but not taken us through it on dry land —
Dayenu, it would have sufficed for us!

If He had taken us through the sea on dry land, but not drowned our oppressors in it —
Dayenu, it would have sufficed for us!

If He had drowned our oppressors in it, but not supplied our needs in the desert for forty years —
Dayenu, it would have sufficed for us!

If He had supplied our needs in the desert for forty years, but not fed us the manna —
Dayenu, it would have sufficed for us!

If He had fed us the manna, but not given us the Sabbath —
Dayenu, it would have sufficed for us!

If He had given us the Sabbath, but not led us to Mount Sinai —
Dayenu, it would have sufficed for us!

If He had led us to Mount Sinai, but not given us the *Torah* —
Dayenu, it would have sufficed for us!

If He had given us the *Torah*, but not brought us into the land of Israel —
Dayenu, it would have sufficed for us!

If He had brought us into the land of Israel, but not built for us the Holy Temple —
Dayenu, it would have sufficed for us!

READER: Therefore, how much more so should we be grateful to the Omnipresent One for all His manifold favors! He brought us out of Egypt, and carried out judgments against them, and against their idols, and smote their firstborn, and gave us their wealth, and split the sea for us, and took us through it on dry land, and drowned our oppressors in it, and supplied our needs in the desert for forty years, and fed us the manna, and gave us the Sabbath, and led us to Mount Sinai, and gave us the *Torah*, and brought us into the land of Israel, and built the Holy Temple for us to atone for all our sins.

COMMENTARY ON "DAYENU!"

Just as we appreciated all the actions that God took against our enemy in our favor, we now take the time to recognize all the many miracles that He did directly for our benefit. The purpose of Dayenu *is to teach us to focus on how God has met our every need. At times, we forget and take things for granted. Here, we appreciate each and every favor that God did and proclaim, "It would have sufficed for us!" Any of these miracles would have been reason enough to be thankful. Taken together, we are overwhelmed with gratitude for the multitude of miracles that we have received and continue to receive because of God's lovingkindness that never fails.*

PASSOVER, MATZAH, AND MAROR

We now speak about three key elements of the Passover Seder. *As we discuss each item, we look at it and then speak about its significance.*

READER: Rabbi Gamaliel used to say: Whoever does not discuss the following three things on Passover has not fulfilled his duty, namely: Passover (the Passover sacrifice); *matzah* (the unleavened bread); and *maror* (the bitter herbs).

Look at the bone on the seder *plate and say:*

READER: This Passover sacrifice that our fathers ate during the time of the Holy Temple — for what reason did they eat it?
   Because the Omnipresent passed over our fathers' houses in Egypt, as it is said: *"Then tell them, 'It is the Passover sacrifice to the* LORD*, who passed over the houses of the Israelites in Egypt and spared our homes when he struck down the Egyptians.' Then the people bowed down and worshiped"* (Exodus 12:27).

COMMENTARY ON "PASSOVER, MATZAH, AND MAROR"

As the storytelling portion of the night comes to an end, we make sure that we haven't left anything out. Rabbi Gamaliel tells us that there are three items that are so essential to the telling of the Exodus story that if we haven't touched upon all of them, our Seder *is incomplete. As opposed to other* seder *elements that are not derived from the Bible, these three items are each mentioned in the Bible as separate commandments (Exodus 12:27, Deuteronomy 5:15 and 16:3). These three items were also eaten together on the eve of the Exodus as they were commanded:* "That same night they are to eat the meat roasted over the fire, along with bitter herbs, and bread made without yeast" *(Exodus 12:8). Together, these three items symbolize the three core ideas of Passover – the bitterness of oppression, faith in God, and salvation. It is only when we mention all three that our Passover service is complete.*

Hold up the broken middle matzah *for all to see and say:*

READER: This *matzah* that we eat — for what reason do we eat it?

   Because the dough of our fathers did not have time to become leavened before the King of kings, the Holy One, blessed be He, revealed Himself to them and redeemed them. As it is said: *"With the dough the Israelites had brought from Egypt, they baked loaves of unleavened bread. The dough was without yeast because they had been driven out of Egypt and did not have time to prepare food for themselves"* (Exodus 12:39).

Hold up the maror *for all to see and say:*

READER: This *maror* that we eat – for what reason do we eat it?

   Because the Egyptians embittered our fathers' lives in Egypt, as it is said: *"They made their lives bitter with harsh labor in brick and mortar and with all kinds of work in the fields; in all their harsh labor the Egyptians worked them ruthlessly"* (Exodus 1:14).

Matzah *and* maror

61

IN EVERY GENERATION

READER: In every generation a person is obligated to regard himself as if he had come out of Egypt, as it is said: *"On that day tell your son, 'I do this because of what the LORD did for me when I came out of Egypt'"* (Exodus 13:8).

The Holy One, blessed be He, redeemed not only our fathers from Egypt, but He also redeemed us with them, as it is said: *"But he brought us out from there to bring us in and give us the land he promised on oath to our ancestors"* (Deuteronomy 6:23).

COMMENTARY ON "IN EVERY GENERATION"

At this point we conclude the storytelling portion of the Seder *and move on to offering thanks and praise. However, first we recognize that the whole point of the* Seder, *with all of the rituals and readings, is so that we can re-live the actual Exodus. We need to reach the point where we feel as though we were personally redeemed by God so that we will internalize the same lessons and integrate the same messages that the ancient Israelites received as they left Egypt thousands of years ago. We need to make the story authentic so that our spiritual transformation can also be real and lasting.*

THANKS AND PRAISE

Cover the matzah *and raise the cup. The cup is held throughout this section of praises until we reach the blessing over the second cup of wine.*

READER: Therefore, it is our duty to thank, to laud, to praise, to glorify, to exalt, to adore, to bless, to elevate, and to honor the One who did all these miracles for our fathers and for us. He took us from slavery to freedom, from sorrow to joy, and from mourning to festivity, and from deep darkness to great light, and from bondage to redemption! Therefore, let us recite a new song before Him. Hallelujah!

ALL: [Read Psalm 113]

Praise the LORD.

Praise the LORD, you his servants;
* praise the name of the LORD.*
Let the name of the LORD be praised,
* both now and forevermore.*
From the rising of the sun to the place
*   where it sets,*
*   the name of the LORD is to be praised.*

The LORD is exalted over all the nations,
* his glory above the heavens.*
Who is like the LORD our God,
* the One who sits enthroned on high,*

who stoops down to look
* on the heavens and the earth?*

He raises the poor from the dust
* and lifts the needy from the ash heap;*
he seats them with princes,
* with the princes of his people.*
He settles the childless woman in her home
* as a happy mother of children.*

Praise the LORD.

ALL: [Read Psalm 114]

When Israel came out of Egypt,
* Jacob from a people of foreign tongue,*
Judah became God's sanctuary,
* Israel his dominion.*

The sea looked and fled,
* the Jordan turned back;*
the mountains leaped like rams,
* the hills like lambs.*

Why was it, sea, that you fled?
* Why, Jordan, did you turn back?*
Why, mountains, did you leap like rams,
* you hills, like lambs?*

Tremble, earth, at the presence of the Lord,
* at the presence of the God of Jacob,*
who turned the rock into a pool,
* the hard rock into springs of water.*

READER: Blessed are You, LORD, our God, King of the universe, who has redeemed us and redeemed our fathers from Egypt, and enabled us to attain this night to eat *matzah* and *maror*. So too, LORD, our God and God of our fathers, bring us to future holidays and festivals that may come to us in peace, when we shall rejoice in the rebuilding of Your city, and shall be joyful in Your Temple service. Then we shall eat of the sacrifices and of the Passover-offering whose blood shall be sprinkled on the wall of Your altar for acceptance; and we shall thank You with a new song for our redemption and for the deliverance of our souls. Blessed are You, LORD, who has redeemed Israel.

Recite the following blessing, and drink the second cup of wine while reclining.

ALL: Blessed are You, LORD, our God, King of the universe, who creates the fruit of the vine.

COMMENTARY ON "THANKS AND PRAISE"

This section begins with the word "Therefore," which connects it to the previous section where we discussed the importance of feeling as if we have personally been delivered from Egypt. The idea is that when we feel as though we ourselves have just received a great miracle, we will be moved to offer genuine and heartfelt praise, which we do in this section. Our storytelling has melded into giving thanks and praise to God since by telling the story we see His hand in our salvation, and we witness His goodness, kindness, power, and justice. We conclude the storytelling section by blessing the second cup of wine and drinking it. We are now ready to proceed to the next step of the Seder.

6. *RACHTZAH* — HAND WASHING WITH A BLESSING

As opposed to the hand washing that we did earlier in the Seder, this time, everyone participates in the ritual hand washing. We pour water from a cup, first twice on the right hand and then twice on the left. Each individual recites the following blessing after washing and then remains silent until after the blessings on the matzah have been said and matzah has been eaten.

ALL: Blessed are You, LORD, our God, King of the universe, who has sanctified us with His commandments and commanded us concerning the washing of the hands.

Pilate Washing His Hands (detail), by Hendrick ter Brugghen, between 1615 and 1628, oil on canvas, 103 x 139 cm, bequeathed by J. A. D. Shipley, 1909

COMMENTARY ON *RACHTZAH*

In the Jewish tradition, we wash our hands every time before we eat a meal. Technically, the rabbis considered food to be a meal only when it includes bread, and so the prevailing custom is to wash our hands whenever we are about to consume any type of bread, including matzah. *As the act of eating is primarily a physical act, in Jewish thought it is considered something that brings us down to the level of an animal who behaves according to its desires and instincts alone.*

When we wash our hands, we cleanse ourselves of this purely physical behavior and prepare ourselves for an act of holiness. Eating can become a holy act when we eat for the sake of taking care of our bodies so that we can better serve God. As we sanctify our hands, we are, in essence, proclaiming the intention that all our actions, including eating and enjoying our food, be infused with spiritual meaning and holiness.

On Passover night, this act takes on special significance — it is an expression of freedom and a demonstration that we are not enslaved by our body and its desires; rather, we are a master over them.

COMMENTARY ON *MOTZI-MATZAH*

The first blessing we recite is the blessing that we say year-round when eating any type of bread. This is the "motzi" step of the Seder, *which means "brings forth," as in "who brings forth bread of the earth." The question the sages ask is: Why do we bless God as the One who brings forth bread of the earth? God gives us wheat from the earth, but humans make the bread! The answer is that even our ability to make bread – our intellect and resources – are all gifts from God. This blessing celebrates humanity's God-given ability to become master over the world by transforming natural resources into something better. We are grateful for the freedom and ability to create.*

The second blessing is the "matzah" section of the Seder. *As you probably recall,* matzah *is the symbol of both our affliction as the poor man's bread and also of our redemption that came suddenly with no time for the bread to rise. Both conditions were perfectly orchestrated by God for our greater good. While the* motzi *blessing celebrates the ability of humanity to create and improve God's world, the blessing of* matzah *reminds us that no matter how great our efforts and abilities, God is the ultimate Creator and Master of the world.*

True freedom is when we are able to let go of the need to control everything and remain calm in any situation because we know that God is in complete control and that everything is exactly as it should be.

7 & 8. *MOTZI-MATZAH* — BLESSING AND EATING THE *MATZAH*

These two steps are almost one as we perform them back to back with no pause in between. First, we hold the matzot *in the order that they are lying on the tray — the broken piece between the two whole* matzot *– and recite the following blessing:*

LEADER: Blessed are You, LORD, our God, King of the universe, who brings forth bread from the earth.

ALL: Amen

Next, we put down the third matzah *(the bottom one), and recite the following blessing over the broken* matzah *and the top one:*

LEADER: Blessed are You, LORD, our God, King of the universe, who has sanctified us with His commandments and commanded us concerning the eating of* matzah.

ALL: Amen

Now we break the matzah *into pieces and everyone eats some of the blessed* matzah *while reclining to the left. The additional* matzot *on the table can also be eaten at this time, but make sure to save some for the next steps.*

9. MAROR — EATING THE BITTER HERBS

Take some of the bitter herbs or vegetable, dip it into the haroset *mixture, and recite the following blessing. Then eat the bitter herbs without reclining, as this is a symbol of slavery and not of freedom.*

ALL: Blessed are You, LORD, our God, King of the universe, who has sanctified us with His commandments and commanded us concerning the eating of *maror*.

COMMENTARY ON MAROR

On Passover night, we are commanded not only to celebrate the Exodus from Egypt, but also to eat bitter herbs in remembrance of the Egyptian slavery. We dip the bitter herbs in the haroset *mixture, which is meant to look like the mortar the Israelite slaves were forced to use in making bricks to build Egyptian cities. However, the* haroset *is also sweet, which reminds us that there is a "sweetness" to our suffering even as it is bitter and harsh.*

God does not allow suffering for no reason. Rather, our suffering plays a key part in our redemption. The sages refer to Egypt to as kur habarzel, *the iron crucible. Just as a crucible purifies silver, our difficulties are meant to refine us. Many people are imprisoned by a victim mentality – one that tells us that we are limited or damaged by our circumstances. On Passover, we assert our freedom by celebrating our bitter times as we recognize that they, too, are gifts from God that help us grow, change, and thrive.*

10. KORECH —
HILLEL'S SANDWICH

*T*ake some of the bitter vegetable along with a bit of the haroset *mixture and place it in between two pieces of* matzah *(the leader should use the third of the ceremonial* matzot *for this purpose). Then recite the following and eat the sandwich in a reclining position:*

ALL: This is what Hillel did at the time when the Holy Temple stood: He would combine the Passover lamb, *matzah*, and *maror*, and eat them together, as it is said: *"They are to eat the lamb, together with unleavened bread and bitter herbs"* (Numbers 9:11).

COMMENTARY ON *KORECH*

Hillel was a great sage who lived during the times when the Temple stood in Jerusalem and the Passover sacrifice was brought there every year on Passover. Hillel initiated a practice where one would combine all of the main Passover elements – the Passover lamb, matzah, *and* maror *–into one sandwich. What is the symbolism of this combination? The bitter herbs represent the bitterness of slavery, the Passover lamb represents redemption, and the* matzah *is a symbol of both slavery and redemption. By placing these items together, Hillel made a very profound statement: Oppression and redemption are all part of the same process. Our trials and our salvation are not two separate experiences without any connection to each other; rather, they are but two sides of the very same coin, and one does not exist without the other.*

11. *SHULCHAN ORECH* — EATING THE MEAL

At this point we partake of the festive holiday meal. It is customary to begin with a peeled hardboiled egg in saltwater.

COMMENTARY ON *SHULCHAN ORECH*

It's important to note that the festive meal is not a "break" from the Seder; rather, it is an integral part of the Seder and one of the fifteen steps toward freedom. The addiction to materialism and the human drive toward physical pleasures has the potential to enslave us and prevent us from living how we truly would like to live. However, according to Judaism, the solution is not to escape the material world, but rather to embrace our physical needs and elevate them for holy purposes.

During the festive meal, we practice this principle as we serve a delicious meal in the most elegant way possible and truly enjoy the experience. At the same time, we are clear that the purpose of the meal is to celebrate God's salvation and, in this way, our festivities become a vehicle through which we connect to God.

There are several reasons given for beginning the meal with a hardboiled egg. The first draws on the use of an egg as the traditional food for mourners. In the Jewish tradition, it is the first thing that a mourner eats after a burial. On Passover night, we remember that while we celebrate God's miraculous salvation for the Jewish people from Egypt, we still mourn the destruction of the Holy Temple in Jerusalem and pray that it be rebuilt speedily with even more miracles. In addition, according to Jewish tradition, our father Abraham passed away on the same night as Passover, and we recall his passing through eating this "mourner's food."

Second, an egg symbolizes birth. It is a source of renewal and new life. In this context, the egg reminds us that Passover is a time of rejuvenation. It marks the birth of the nation of Israel and carries with it an intrinsic power for all people to grow, change, and be spiritually reborn on this holiday. Just as nature comes back to life in the springtime, during the season of Passover, all human beings can blossom, bloom, and thrive at this time.

Finally, the egg symbolizes resilience and strength in the face of adversity. When every other type of food is placed inside a pot of boiling water, the food typically becomes soft. The egg, on the other hand, only becomes harder the longer that it is cooked. Similarly, the children of Israel were "cooked and boiled" by the Egyptians, but it only served to make them stronger. Likewise, during Passover and throughout the year, we try to integrate that kind of resilience and faith into our own lives.

12. TZAFUN — EATING THE *AFIKOMEN*

*E*arlier in the evening we broke the middle *matzah and put aside the larger half for later. Now we take out that half of matzah, divide it between participants, and eat it. This piece of matzah is called the afikomen and is known as the Passover "dessert." It is the last thing that we eat and nothing at all should be had afterward, except for the two remaining cups of wine, water, or tea. We eat the afikomen while reclining.*

COMMENTARY ON *TZAFUN*

The main reason for eating the afikomen *at this point is in remembrance of the Passover sacrifice that was eaten on this night during Temple times. While we no longer can eat from that offering, we can eat the* matzah *that was traditionally eaten with the meat of the sacrifice. It is the last thing that we eat because we want the taste to linger in our mouths. Symbolically, we want the message of the* matzah *to last long after the* Seder *has concluded.*

There is a deeper meaning to this step as well. The word tzafun *means "hidden." This half of* matzah, *which was hidden for most of the evening but is now revealed, is symbolic of the hidden future that awaits us all. A large step in freedom is recognizing that our current situation is not our final destination, even if our destiny remains concealed from our eyes. We are no longer prisoners of our present circumstances when we recognize that God is in control and that He can change everything in an instant and bring about salvation.*

13. *BARECH* — BLESSING AFTER EATING

*W*e *pour the third cup for each other and then recite the traditional Grace After Meals over the cup of wine.*

ALL: [Read Psalm 126]

> When the LORD restored the fortunes
>   of Zion,
>   we were like those who dreamed.
> Our mouths were filled with laughter,
>   our tongues with songs of joy.
> Then it was said among the nations,
>   "The LORD has done great things for
>   them."
> The LORD has done great things for us,
>   and we are filled with joy.
>
> Restore our fortunes, LORD,
>   like streams in the Negev.
> Those who sow with tears
>   will reap with songs of joy.
> Those who go out weeping,
>   carrying seed to sow,
> will return with songs of joy,
>   carrying sheaves with them.

LEADER: Let us say Grace!

ALL: Blessed be the Name of God, now and forevermore!

LEADER: With your permission, let us praise God from whose store we have eaten!

ALL: Blessed be our God from whose store we have eaten and through whose goodness we live.

LEADER: Blessed be our God from whose store we have eaten and through whose goodness we live.

ALL: Blessed be He, and blessed be His Name: Blessed are You, LORD, our God, King of the universe, who, in His goodness, feeds the whole world with grace, with kindness and with mercy. He gives food to all flesh, for His kindness is everlasting. Through His great goodness to us continuously we do not lack food, and may we never lack it, for the sake of His great Name. For He is a benevolent God who feeds and sustains all, does good to all, and prepares food for all His creatures whom He has created, as it is said: *"You open your hand and satisfy the desires of every living thing"* (Psalm 145:16). Blessed are You LORD, who provides food for all.

We thank You, LORD, our God, for having given as a heritage to our fathers a precious, good, and spacious land; for having brought us out, LORD our God, from the land of Egypt and redeemed us from the house of slaves; for Your covenant which You have sealed in our flesh; for Your *Torah* which You have taught us; for Your statutes which You have made known to us; for the life, favor, and kindness which You have graciously bestowed upon us; and for the food we eat with which You constantly feed and sustain us every day, at all times, and at every hour.

For all this, LORD our God, we thank You and bless You. May Your Name be blessed by the mouth of every living being, constantly and forever. As it is written: *"When you have eaten and*

are satisfied, praise the LORD your God for the good land he has given you" (Deuteronomy 8:10). Blessed are You, LORD, for the land and for the food.

Have mercy, LORD our God, upon Israel Your people, upon Jerusalem Your city, upon Zion the abode of Your glory, upon the kingship of the house of David Your anointed, and upon the great and holy House which is called by Your Name. Our God, our Father, our Shepherd, feed us, sustain us, nourish us and give us comfort; and speedily, LORD our God, grant us relief from all our afflictions. LORD, our God, please do not make us dependent upon the gifts of mortal men nor upon their loans, but only upon Your full, open, holy, and generous hand, that we may not be shamed or disgraced forever and ever.

The following paragraph, special for Passover, is said here:

Our God and God of our fathers, may there ascend, come and reach, be seen and accepted, heard, recalled, and re-membered before You, the remembrance and recollection of us, the remembrance of our fathers, the remembrance of the Messiah, the son of David Your servant, the remembrance of Jerusalem Your holy city, and the remembrance of all Your people the House of Israel, for deliverance, well-being, grace, kindness, mercy, good life and peace, on this day of the Festival of *Matzot*, on this Festival of holy convocation. Remember us on this day, LORD, our God, for good; recollect us on this day for blessing; help us on this day for good life. With the promise of deliverance and compassion, spare us and be gracious to us; have mercy upon us and deliver us; for our eyes are directed to You, for You, God, are a gracious and merciful King.

Rebuild Jerusalem the holy city speedily in our days. Blessed are You, LORD, who in His mercy rebuilds Jerusalem. Amen

Blessed are You, LORD, our God, King of the universe, benevolent God, our Father, our King, our Might, our Creator, our Redeemer, our Maker, our Holy One, the Holy One of Jacob, our Shepherd, the Shepherd of Israel, the King who is good and does good to all, each and every day. He has done good for us, He does good for us, and He will do good for us; He has bestowed, He bestows, and He will forever bestow upon us grace, kindness and mercy, relief, salvation and success, blessing and help, consolation, sustenance and nourishment, compassion, life, peace and all goodness; and may He never cause us to lack any good.

May the Merciful One reign over us forever and ever.

May the Merciful One be blessed in heaven and on earth.

May the Merciful One be praised for all generations, and be glorified in us forever and all eternity, and honored in us forever and ever.

May the Merciful One sustain us with honor.

May the Merciful One break the yoke of exile from our neck and may He lead us upright to our land.

May the Merciful One send abundant blessing into this house and upon this table at which we have eaten.

May the Merciful One send us Elijah the Prophet. May he be remembered for good and may he bring us good tidings, salvation, and consolation.

May the Merciful One bless all who are present here along with us and all that is ours. Just as He blessed our forefathers, Abraham, Isaac and Jacob, "in everything," "from everything," "with everything," so may He bless all of us together with a perfect blessing, and let us say, Amen.

O, may their merits and our merits be pleaded in heaven to assure peace. May we receive blessing from the LORD and just kindness from the God of our salvation, and may we find grace and good understanding in the eyes of God and man.

May the Merciful One cause us to inherit that day which is all good.

May the Merciful One grant us the privilege of reaching the days of the Messiah and the life of the world to come. He is a tower of salvation to His king, and bestows kindness upon His anointed, to David and his descendants forever. He who makes peace in His heights, may He make peace for us and for all Israel; and say, Amen.

Fear the LORD, you His holy ones, for those who fear Him suffer no want. Young lions are in need and go hungry, but those who seek the LORD shall not lack any good. Give thanks to the LORD for He is good, for His kindness is everlasting.

You open Your hand and satisfy the desire of every living thing. Blessed is the man who trusts in the LORD, and the LORD will be his trust. I was young and now I have grown old, yet never have I seen a righteous man abandoned nor his children begging for bread. The LORD will give strength to His people, the LORD will bless His people with peace!

Recite the following blessing, and drink the third cup of wine while reclining.

ALL: Blessed are You, LORD, our God, King of the universe, who creates the fruit of the vine.

COMMENTARY ON *BARECH*

It is a biblical commandment to praise God after we eat any meal all year long: "When you have eaten and are satisfied, praise the LORD your God for the good land he has given you" *(Deuteronomy 8:10). We are to see every single meal as no less significant than the manna that fell daily from the sky during the forty years that the children of Israel spent in the desert, and we are to be as grateful for our daily food. If this commandment is essential every day of the year, how much more so on* seder *night when the whole focus of the evening is recognizing and giving thanks for all God's miracles that He lovingly bestows upon us. When we are cognizant of the fact that God – and not humans – is the source of all our blessings, we take another step toward freedom. We need not serve people or ideals; we serve God alone for He is our true Provider.*

The Grace After Meals text was composed over a long period of time by different people. According to Jewish tradition, Moses composed the first paragraph that concludes, "Blessed are You LORD, who provides food for all" after the manna was given in the desert. Joshua composed the next two paragraphs, which conclude, "Blessed are You, LORD, for the land and for the food" when Israel first entered the Holy Land.

David and Solomon, who conquered and built Jerusalem, authored the sections concluding with, "Blessed are You, LORD, who in His mercy rebuilds Jerusalem." However, these sections were changed after the exile to reflect the new circumstances. During the exile, the rest of the text was included and Psalm 126 was placed as an introduction. These amendments were initiated in order to place the longing for the land of Israel and redemption at the forefront of everyone's minds – even after just eating a satisfying meal. On all nights, and especially on Passover night, we remember that our redemption is not yet complete, and we long for our full salvation.

14. *HALLEL* — SONGS OF PRAISE

The fourth cup of wine is filled, as well as the Cup of Elijah. We open the door to the house to invite Elijah into our homes and recite the following verses, after which we close the door again.

ALL: *"Pour out your wrath on the nations that do not acknowledge you, on the kingdoms that do not call on your name; for they have devoured Jacob and devastated his homeland"* (Psalm 79:6–7). *"Pour out your wrath on them; let your fierce anger overtake them"* (Psalm 69:24). *"Pursue them in anger and destroy them from under the heavens of the LORD"* (Lamentations 3:66).

Now we recite the psalms and prayers that form the traditional praise and thanksgiving liturgy.

ALL: [Read Psalm 115]

*Not to us, LORD, not to us
   but to your name be the glory, because
    of your love and faithfulness.*

*Why do the nations say,
   "Where is their God?"
Our God is in heaven;
   he does whatever pleases him.*

*But their idols are silver and gold,
   made by human hands.
They have mouths, but cannot speak,
   eyes, but cannot see.
They have ears, but cannot hear,
   noses, but cannot smell.
They have hands, but cannot feel,
   feet, but cannot walk,
    nor can they utter a sound with their
     throats.
Those who make them will be like
   them,
   and so will all who trust in them.*

*All you Israelites, trust in the LORD—
   he is their help and shield.
House of Aaron, trust in the LORD—
   he is their help and shield.
You who fear him, trust in the LORD—
   he is their help and shield.*

*The LORD remembers us and will bless us:
   He will bless his people Israel,
   he will bless the house of Aaron,
he will bless those who fear the LORD—
   small and great alike.*

*May the LORD cause you to flourish,
   both you and your children.
May you be blessed by the LORD,
   the Maker of heaven and earth.*

The highest heavens belong to the LORD,
  but the earth he has given to mankind.
It is not the dead who praise the LORD,
  those who go down to the place of
    silence;
it is we who extol the LORD,
  both now and forevermore.

Praise the LORD.

Creation Day

ALL: [Read Psalm 116]

I love the LORD, for he heard my voice;
  he heard my cry for mercy.
Because he turned his ear to me,
  I will call on him as long as I live.

The cords of death entangled me,
  the anguish of the grave came over me;
  I was overcome by distress and sorrow.
Then I called on the name of the LORD:
  "LORD, save me!"

The LORD is gracious and righteous;
  our God is full of compassion.
The LORD protects the unwary;
  when I was brought low, he saved me.

Return to your rest, my soul,
  for the LORD has been good to you.

For you, LORD, have delivered me from
    death,
  my eyes from tears,
  my feet from stumbling,
that I may walk before the LORD
  in the land of the living.

I trusted in the LORD when I said,
  "I am greatly afflicted";
in my alarm I said,
  "Everyone is a liar."

What shall I return to the LORD
  for all his goodness to me?

I will lift up the cup of salvation
  and call on the name of the LORD.
I will fulfill my vows to the LORD
  in the presence of all his people.

Precious in the sight of the LORD
   is the death of his faithful servants.
Truly I am your servant, LORD;
   I serve you just as my mother did;
   you have freed me from my chains.

I will sacrifice a thank offering to you
   and call on the name of the LORD.
I will fulfill my vows to the LORD
   in the presence of all his people,
in the courts of the house of the LORD—
   in your midst, Jerusalem.

Praise the LORD.

Noah's thanksgiving

ALL: [Read Psalm 117]

Praise the LORD, all you nations;
   extol him, all you peoples.
For great is his love toward us,
   and the faithfulness of the LORD endures
     forever.

Praise the LORD.

ALL: [Read Psalm 118]

Give thanks to the LORD, for he is good;
   his love endures forever.

Let Israel say:
   "His love endures forever."
Let the house of Aaron say:
   "His love endures forever."
Let those who fear the LORD say:
   "His love endures forever."

When hard pressed, I cried to the LORD;
   he brought me into a spacious place.
The LORD is with me; I will not be afraid.
   What can mere mortals do to me?
The LORD is with me; he is my helper.
   I look in triumph on my enemies.

It is better to take refuge in the LORD
   than to trust in humans.
It is better to take refuge in the LORD
   than to trust in princes.
All the nations surrounded me,

but in the name of the LORD I cut them
    down.
They surrounded me on every side,
    but in the name of the LORD I cut them
    down.
They swarmed around me like bees,
    but they were consumed as quickly as
      burning thorns;
    in the name of the LORD I cut them down.
I was pushed back and about to fall,
    but the LORD helped me.
The LORD is my strength and my defense;
    he has become my salvation.

Shouts of joy and victory
    resound in the tents of the righteous:
"The LORD's right hand has done mighty
    things!
    The LORD's right hand is lifted high;
    the LORD's right hand has done mighty
      things!"
I will not die but live,
    and will proclaim what the LORD has
      done.
The LORD has chastened me severely,
    but he has not given me over to death.
Open for me the gates of the righteous;
    I will enter and give thanks to the LORD.
This is the gate of the LORD
    through which the righteous may enter.
I will give you thanks, for you
      answered me;
    you have become my salvation.

The stone the builders rejected
    has become the cornerstone;
the LORD has done this,
    and it is marvelous in our eyes.
The LORD has done it this very day;
    let us rejoice today and be glad.

LORD, save us!
    LORD, grant us success!

Blessed is he who comes in the name of the
    LORD.
    From the house of the LORD we bless you.
The LORD is God,
    and he has made his light shine on us.
With boughs in hand, join in the festal
    procession
    up to the horns of the altar.

You are my God, and I will praise you;
    you are my God, and I will exalt you.

Give thanks to the LORD, for he is good;
    his love endures forever.

LEADER: LORD, our God, all Your works
shall praise You; Your pious ones, the
righteous who do Your will, and all Your
people, the House of Israel, with joyous
song will thank and bless, laud and glorify, exalt and adore, sanctify and proclaim
the sovereignty of Your Name, our King.
For it is good to thank You, and befitting to sing to Your Name, for from the

beginning to the end of the world You are Almighty God. Give thanks to the LORD, for He is good for His kindness is everlasting.

David repents.

ALL: [Read Psalm 136]

Give thanks to the LORD, for he is good.
  His love endures forever.
Give thanks to the God of gods.
  His love endures forever.
Give thanks to the Lord of lords:
  His love endures forever.

to him who alone does great wonders,
  His love endures forever.
who by his understanding made the heavens,
  His love endures forever.

who spread out the earth upon the waters,
  His love endures forever.
who made the great lights—
  His love endures forever.
the sun to govern the day,
  His love endures forever.
the moon and stars to govern the night;
  His love endures forever.

to him who struck down the firstborn of Egypt
  His love endures forever.
and brought Israel out from among them
  His love endures forever.
with a mighty hand and outstretched arm;
  His love endures forever.

to him who divided the Red Sea asunder
  His love endures forever.
and brought Israel through the midst of it,
  His love endures forever.
but swept Pharaoh and his army into the Red Sea;
  His love endures forever.

to him who led his people through the wilderness;
  His love endures forever.

to him who struck down great kings,
  His love endures forever.
and killed mighty kings—
  His love endures forever.

Sihon king of the Amorites
  His love endures forever.
and Og king of Bashan—
  His love endures forever.
and gave their land as an inheritance,
  His love endures forever.
an inheritance to his servant Israel.
  His love endures forever.

He remembered us in our low estate
  His love endures forever.
and freed us from our enemies.
  His love endures forever.
He gives food to every creature.
  His love endures forever.

Give thanks to the God of heaven.
  His love endures forever.

Ezra reads the book of the Law.

LEADER: The soul of every living being shall bless Your Name, LORD, our God; and the spirit of all flesh shall always glorify and exalt Your remembrance, our King. From the beginning to the end of the world You are Almighty God; and other than You we have no King, Redeemer and Savior who delivers, rescues, sustains, answers and is merciful in every time of trouble and distress; we have no King but You.

You are the God of the first and of the last generations, God of all creatures, LORD of all events, who is extolled with manifold praises, who directs His world with kindness and His creatures with compassion. Behold, the LORD neither slumbers nor sleeps. He arouses the sleepers and awakens the slumberous, gives speech to the mute, releases the bound, supports the falling and raises up those who are bowed.

To You alone we give thanks. Even if our mouths were filled with song as the sea, and our tongues with joyous singing like the multitudes of its waves, and our lips with praise like the expanse of the sky; and our eyes shining like the sun and the moon, and our hands spread out like the eagles of heaven, and our feet swift like deer we would still be unable to thank You LORD, our God and God of our fathers, and to bless Your Name, for even one of the thousands of millions, and myriads of myriads, of favors, miracles and wonders which You have done for us and for our fathers before us.

LORD, our God, You have redeemed us from Egypt, You have freed us from the house of bondage, You have fed us in famine and nourished us in plenty; You have saved us from the sword and delivered us from pestilence, and raised us from evil and lasting maladies. Until now Your mercies have helped us, and Your kindnesses have not forsaken us; and do not abandon us, LORD our God, forever! Therefore, the limbs which You have arranged within us, and the spirit and soul which You have breathed into our nostrils, and the tongue which You have placed in our mouth they all shall thank, bless, praise, glorify, exalt, adore, sanctify and proclaim the sovereignty of Your Name, our King.

For every mouth shall offer thanks to You, every tongue shall swear by You, every eye shall look to You, every knee shall bend to You, all who stand erect shall bow down before You, all hearts shall fear You, and every innermost part shall sing praise to Your Name, as it is written: *"My whole being will exclaim, 'Who is like you, LORD? You rescue the poor from those too strong for them, the poor and needy from those who rob them'"* (Psalm 35:10).

Psalmist David gives praise and thanks.

Who can be likened to You, who is equal to You, who can be compared to You, the great, mighty, awesome God, God most high, Possessor of heaven and earth! We will laud You, praise You and glorify You, and we will bless Your holy Name, as it is said: *"Praise the LORD, my soul; all my inmost being, praise his holy name"* (Psalm 103:1).

You are the Almighty God in the power of Your strength; the Great in the glory of Your Name; the Mighty forever, and the Awesome in Your awesome deeds; the King who sits upon a lofty and exalted throne.

He who dwells for eternity, lofty and holy is His Name. And it is written: *"Sing joyfully to the LORD, you righteous; it is fitting for the upright to praise him"* (Psalm 33:1). By the mouth of the upright You are exalted; by the lips of the righteous You are blessed; by the tongue of the pious You are sanctified; and among the holy ones You are praised.

In the assemblies of the myriads of Your people, the House of Israel, Your Name, our King, shall be glorified with song in every generation. For such is the obligation of all creatures before You, LORD, our God and God of our fathers, to thank, to laud, to praise, to glorify, to exalt, to adore, to bless, to elevate and to honor You, even beyond all the words of songs and praises of David son of Jesse, Your anointed servant.

And therefore may Your Name be praised forever, our King, the great and holy God and King in heaven and on earth. For to You, LORD, our God and God of our fathers, forever befits song and praise, laud and hymn, strength and dominion, victory, greatness and might, glory, splendor, holiness and sovereignty; blessings and thanksgivings to Your great and holy Name; from the beginning to the end of the world You are Almighty God. Blessed are You, LORD, Almighty God, King, great and extolled in praises, God of thanksgivings, LORD of wonders, Creator of all souls, Master of all creatures, who takes pleasure in songs of praise; the only King, the Life of all worlds.

Recite the following blessing, and drink the fourth cup of wine while reclining.

ALL: Blessed are You, LORD, our God, King of the universe, who creates the fruit of the vine.

After drinking the fourth cup, we recite the following blessing:

Psalmist David worships.

LEADER: Blessed are You, LORD our God, King of the universe for the vine and the fruit of the vine, for the produce of the field, and for the precious, good, and spacious land which You have favored to give as a heritage to our fathers, to eat of its fruit and be satiated by its goodness. Have mercy, LORD our God, on Israel Your people, on Jerusalem Your city, on Zion the abode of Your glory, on Your altar and on Your Temple. Rebuild Jerusalem, the holy city, speedily in our days, and bring us up into it, and make us rejoice in it, and we will bless You in holiness and purity and remember us for good on this day of the Festival of *Matzot*. For You, LORD, are good and do good to all, and we thank You for the land and for the fruit of the vine. Blessed are You, LORD, for the land and for the fruit of the vine.

ALL: Amen

COMMENTARY ON *HALLEL*

In this section, we pick up where we left off at the end of the Maggid *section. There are five psalms of praise, Psalms 113–118, that were originally sung as the children of Israel crossed the Red Sea and were sung at every significant victory in Jewish history. They were sung by Joshua after he defeated the kings of Canaan, Hezekiah after he defeated Sennacherib, and Mordecai and Esther after they defeated Haman. They are recited every year on holidays and especially on* seder *night. We already recited two of them earlier, and here we sing the rest. What is the difference between the two sections?*

The sages explain that the psalms recited in the Maggid *section reflected our gratitude for the miracles done in the past. In this section, we turn our focus to the future and express our joy and gratitude for all of the miracles yet to come. How liberating it is to go through life knowing that just as God perfectly and lovingly orchestrated history in the past, He is doing so right now in the present and will continue to do so forever. What a wonderful world to live in! For that we express our endless thanks and sing His praises.*

15. *NIRTZAH* —
CONCLUSION OF THE *SEDER*

We declare that the Seder is officially complete and then end the evening with songs that are joyful, playful, and celebrate our core values.

ALL: Our Passover *Seder* is now completed in accordance with all its laws, its ordinances and statutes. Just as we were found worthy to perform it, so may we be worthy to do it in the future. O Pure One, who dwells on high, raise up the congregation, which is without number! Soon, and with rejoicing, lead the offshoots of the stock that You have planted, redeemed, to Zion.

Next year in Jerusalem!

Rebuilding the Jerusalem Temple

COMMENTARY ON *NIRTZAH*

With this short paragraph, our Seder comes to a close. We declare that we have finished the service of the night and express our hope that we can perform the service again next year, preferably in Jerusalem. However, what makes this concluding section a part of the steps toward freedom?

Perhaps the most well-known phrase of the Exodus story is "Let my people go!" Moses says it to Pharaoh over and over again. However, that is only part of the phrase. The whole verse reads: "Let my people go, so that they may worship me" (Exodus 8:1). Service to God is the goal of our freedom, for it is only through serving God and living a life guided by His Word that a person can be truly free.

As we conclude the Seder and prepare to return to our daily lives, we declare that we will take the message of the Seder with us. We will continue to serve and work toward our ultimate goal – a full redemption so that we can serve God in the greatest way possible at the Temple in Jerusalem during the messianic era.

DEVOTIONAL GUIDE

INTRODUCTION

As we have just learned, Passover commemorates the pivotal event in Jewish history — the Exodus of the Israelites from bondage in Egypt. It was at this juncture more than three thousand years ago that the national identity of the Jewish people was truly shaped. And it was from this event that some of the most profound affirmations of the Jewish faith were formed: that God is present in human lives; that He hears the cries of the suffering and persecuted; and that He intervenes in history to deliver humanity from affliction and to redeem us from oppression.

It is out of those deeply held convictions that the Jewish people come to the Passover table each year, as they have done throughout the centuries, to remember and to relive that experience of going from slavery to freedom, from oppression to redemption. These shared beliefs, too, draw Christians to learn more about this biblically mandated holy day that Jesus observed and shared with his disciples during his final meal on earth.

It is with this in mind that Rabbi Eckstein shares his spiritual insights for you to reflect upon during this most holy season for Christians and Jews alike. These devotions and Scripture readings hopefully will expand your understanding of the Passover celebration and its ties to the Christian faith, as well as deepen your spiritual life as you reflect on how God miraculously works in the lives of His people – in the past, in the present, and in the future to come.

Passover Eve
A HOLIDAY CALLED PASSOVER

"The blood will be a sign for you on the houses where you are, and when I see the blood, I will pass over you. No destructive plague will touch you when I strike Egypt." — EXODUS 12:13

The *Torah* reading for today is from Exodus 32:11–34:10.

Perhaps you have wondered why the holiday is called Passover. Sure, we know that the name comes from the plague of the firstborn when the angel of death "passed over" the houses of the Israelites marked with the blood of a sacrificed lamb and only took the Egyptians' firstborns. But that's just one of the many acts of God in the story of the Exodus. Why not call the holiday after the more glamorous miracle of the sea parting? Or maybe we could have called it "Exodus" which captures just about the entire story. Why Passover?

The sages explain that holidays on the Jewish calendar are not just about events that happened in the past; they are about events happening right now in the present – in the world around us and in our own personal lives. There is an energy that permeates every holiday, every year. *Yom Kippur* is a time of forgiveness. *Hanukkah*, a time for miracles. *Purim*, a time of joy and salvation. What's the energy of Passover?

Passover is a time of change.

The name Passover isn't just about an act of God that occurred thousands of years ago. Passover also refers to the actions of man that can and should happen every year during the holiday. All year  long we talk about the changes we'd like to make in our lives; we'd like to become more patient or less angry, we'd like to make more time for prayer and Bible study. Or maybe we'd like to make a major lifestyle change. All year long we talk and we think and we deliberate and we plan. On Passover, it's time to pass over all of the thinking and skip right to the doing. It's time to change.

Remember how *matzah* was invented? God said to the Israelites, "Time to go!" The Israelites replied, "Great. We just need to finish baking the bread, prepare a few things, and..." And God said, "No. It's time to go now!" So the Israelites took their dough and made it into the flat bread we eat on Passover called *matzah*: *"The dough was without yeast because they... did not have time to prepare food for themselves"* (Exodus 12:39).

This is the time of year for doing the things we have been putting off because we didn't have the ingredients just right. If we wait for perfect conditions, we may be waiting forever. It's also no accident the Passover takes place in the springtime. It seems that nature all around us is changing, blooming, and blossoming. It's time for us to blossom, too! So, what are you waiting for? Make that call, make that change, and say "yes" to a new opportunity. It's time to go — now!

Day 1

THANKING GOD FOR UNANSWERED PRAYERS

His sister stood at a distance to see what would happen to him. — EXODUS 2:4

The *Torah* reading for today is from Exodus 12:21–51 and Numbers 28:16–25, and the *Haftorah* is from Joshua 3:5–7; 5:2–6:1, 27.

What if God answered every prayer with a resounding "YES"? Would the world be a better and happier place or a worse one? For example, what if God had answered Miriam's prayer as she stood among the reeds next to the Nile River where her baby brother Moses floated in a basket designed to protect him as he drifted in the water?

As you remember the story, Miriam and her mother had placed Moses in the basket as a last resort. The Egyptians had resolved to kill every single Hebrew baby boy. Miriam and her mother hoped that a non-Egyptian would find the infant and have mercy on him.

Miriam watched to find out her baby brother's fate, and as the sages teach, while she waited, she prayed. "God, please watch over him. Please make sure no Egyptian officials find him." Who should come along but the daughter of Pharaoh himself! The daughter of the very man who proclaimed: *"Every Hebrew boy that is born you must throw into the Nile"* (Exodus 1:22).

Miriam continued to pray: "God, please don't let her see him!" But Pharaoh's daughter did see him and she reached for the basket.

Miriam begged: "Please God, don't let her reach him!" Again, God didn't listen to her. Pharaoh's daughter did reach the basket, and according to tradition, God even performed a miracle to lengthen her arm so that she could reach Moses.

Miriam pleaded: "Oh, God, please make her think that he is ugly and no good." But

Pharaoh's daughter was smitten and she decided to take Moses for her son.

And God said: "Good thing I didn't answer you, Miriam! Had I done what you asked, Moses would have drifted off and drowned. Instead he will grow up in Pharaoh's home where he will become a noble, a leader who can redeem Israel." And indeed he did!

Moses Is Found, *by Julius Schnorr von Carolsfeld (German painter, 1794 - 1872)*

Like Miriam, we don't always get what we pray for. But we always get what we need, and that makes all the difference. When we pray for one thing and we don't get what we asked for, it feels as though one of two things has happened: Either God didn't hear our prayers, or He has denied us a gift. But neither is true. God hears every one of our prayers. Sometimes He says "yes" and other times He says "no." But when God says "no," it's not because He doesn't want us to have good things. When God says "no" to what we asked for, it's because He has something even greater to give us!

When your prayers seem to go unanswered, think of Miriam standing desperately by the Egyptian Nile. Thank God for your unanswered prayers because those are often the greatest gifts of all.

Day 2
THROUGH NARROW STRAITS

"And now the cry of the Israelites has reached me, and I have seen the way the Egyptians are oppressing them." — EXODUS 3:9

The *Torah* reading for today is from Leviticus 22:26–23:44 and Numbers 28:16–25, and the *Haftorah* is from 2 Kings 23:1–9, 21–25.

It seems that more people than ever are stressed these days. Even though we have more time-saving devices and the technology to have many chores done for us automatically, people seem to be more pressured and overwhelmed.

The bad news is that stress takes a toll on us. Scientific research has proven that stress affects our body, mind, and emotions. We are less able to cope with illness or everyday challenges and more likely to forget things and make mistakes. But don't despair! There is some good news, too.

Think about how life for each of us began. We were resting comfortably in our mother's womb, when suddenly, there was pressure and pushing. More than likely we became quite uncomfortable and possibly stressed! The contractions continued until we were pushed through a narrow passageway and out into a new world. The miracle of birth had occurred.

The good news about stress: It can lead us to rebirth and renewal!

The Hebrew word for Egypt is *Mitzrayim*. The word comes from a Hebrew word that means "narrow straits" or "constriction." The sages see Egypt as a narrow place, similar to the birth canal. The children of Israel were stressed, oppressed, compressed, and then literally caught in a narrow place when they found themselves sandwiched between the Egyptians and the Red Sea.

But just like the birth process, the stress and confinement were all part of the plan.

When the Israelites couldn't stand it any longer, they threw up their hands and said, "We are powerless, God, and only You can help!" At that point the sea parted, the Israelites left Egypt behind, and a new nation was birthed.

Passover is a holiday that usually comes along with a fair bit of stress — think of Christmas, times eight, to get an idea of how much food preparation is necessary, how much money is spent, and how much general stress the holiday can create! But the stress is all part of the Passover experience. If handled correctly, it can lead us to our own salvation, our own Exodus from the narrow places in our lives, and our own rebirth.

We get stressed because we feel like life is overwhelming, that we can't handle it all and we can't do it alone. The psalmist says, *"Cast your cares on the LORD and he will sustain you"*

(Psalm 55:22). It's true, we can't handle life alone. Once we realize that only God can help us through, the burden is lifted. Instead of feeling stressed, we can rest, relax, and clear our minds, knowing that everything we accomplish is only possible because of generous help from above. We experience life in a totally new way. We are reborn!

The Crossing of the Red Sea

Day 3

OUR CHILDREN, OUR FUTURE

"In days to come, when your son asks you, 'What does this mean?' say to him, 'With a mighty hand the LORD brought us out of Egypt, out of the land of slavery.'" — EXODUS 13:14

The *Torah* reading for today is from Exodus 13:1–16 and Numbers 28:19–25.

The first night of Passover is filled with excitement as we begin the special meal called the *Seder*. Friends and family gather together as holiday aromas fill the air. In addition to the regular holiday table décor, we add a *seder* plate with six items that will be used or mentioned during the *Seder*. For example, a shank bone represents the Passover sacrifice and bitter herbs symbolize slavery. There is plenty of *matzah* and an assortment of fine wines or rich fruit juice for the "four cups" that we drink during the *Seder*. But even the most exquisite table is incomplete without the main centerpiece: Our children.

The Passover *Seder* is built around the children at the table. The reading of the *haggadah* (the text that accompanies the *Seder*) begins with the recitation of the "four questions." The four questions — which begin "Why is this night different than all other nights?" — traditionally are recited by the youngest child. Questions in general are a major theme of the *Seder*. We do all sorts of unusual things just so the children can ask their favorite question: Why? Why isn't there any bread tonight? Why are we eating bitter herbs? Why are we dipping them in salty water?

Why are we so intent on getting our children to ask questions?

We want them to ask questions so that we can give them the answers. We want our children to be interested in our story so that they will listen to it and make it their own. All year long our children ask us questions — about school, nature, life, whatever comes into their minds. Sometimes we answer, and sometimes we waive them off with the brush of our hand. But on *seder* night we are commanded to answer them. It's these answers that will shape their thoughts, and it's their thoughts that will shape the future.

Rabbi Jonathan Sacks, the former Chief Rabbi of Britain, sums it up this way: "The world we build tomorrow is born in the stories we tell our children today." On Passover, we celebrate freedom. We recount our own journey from bitter slavery to sweet freedom, and we cherish this God-given right. God says, "You want a kind and free world? Teach your children first!" Rabbi Sacks continues, "Politics moves the pieces. Education changes the game."

Recent studies have proven that children are likely to become a reflection of the stories that they hear. So what stories are we telling our children? Make the time to sit with a child and read to him. Read her the stories of the Bible or some of the many children's storybooks that exhibit values such as kindness and faith. Today's children are tomorrow's leaders. Let's teach them right.

Day 4
THE OVERFLOWING CUP

*"I am the LORD your God, who brought you
out of Egypt, out of the land of slavery."*
— EXODUS 20:2

The *Torah* reading for today is from
Exodus 22:24–23:19 and Numbers 28:19–25.

Are you a pessimist or an optimist? Believe it or not, one day, according to Jewish tradition, God will want to know.

The sages teach that there are a series of questions each person is asked when his or her time on Earth has come to an end. Among those questions are "were you an honest person?" and "did you make time to study God's Word?" One of them is also "did you anticipate salvation?" In other words, were you an optimist? Did you anticipate that things could get better and that God would help you?

You may wonder if that is really fair? How can God expect us to have a rosy outlook on life all the time? We all know people who seem to be born that way – always smiling, always with a cheerful disposition. But then there are some who seemingly have been born on the opposite end of the spectrum. As one person once said, "I don't just see

the glass as half-empty instead of half-full. I see the glass as half-empty and worry that someone is going to come along and knock it over!" Some of us are just drawn toward thinking negatively. Is that really a crime?

The sages teach, according to the First Commandment, the answer is yes!

Remember the First Commandment in its entirety? *"I am the LORD your God, who brought you out of Egypt, out of the land of slavery"* (Exodus 20:2). More importantly, think about what is not said in this commandment. God

just as the Creator of the world, but as the Savior of our individual lives!

We are commanded to believe in a God who hears our prayers and cares deeply for us. We are instructed to believe in a God who can and will help us out of our own personal bondage, our own trials and difficulties. So can God command us to be optimistic about life? Yes, because to believe in the God who took the Israelites out of Egypt is to believe that God can perform miracles for us, too! He expects that level of faith and commitment from us.

does *not* refer to Himself as the Creator of the world, even though that might have been a more obvious choice. Instead, He commands that we know Him as the God who brought the children of Israel out of Egypt. Why? Because we are commanded to know God not

So next time you come across that proverbial glass, don't see it as half-empty or even as half-full. See it as filling up and believe that it will run over! As it says in Psalm 23: *"my cup overflows"* (v.5).

Day 5

A STORY OF REDEMPTION

The LORD said, "I have indeed seen the misery of my people in Egypt. I have heard them crying out because of their slave drivers, and I am concerned about their suffering. So I have come down to rescue them from the hand of the Egyptians and to bring them up out of that land into a good and spacious land . . . ." — EXODUS 3:7–8

The *Torah* reading for today is from Exodus 33:12–34:26 and Numbers 28:19–25, and the *Haftorah* is from Ezekiel 37:1–14.

Passover, or *Pesach* in Hebrew, commemorates the most influential event in Jewish history — the Exodus of the people of Israel from bondage in Egypt. It was at that particular juncture some three thousand years ago that the national Jewish identity was shaped, and it was from this event that some of the most profound affirmations of the Jewish faith were drawn.

Primary among them is the notion that God is not some distant power, uninterested in His creation. No, the story of Passover affirms for Jewish people that God is present in human life, that He hears the cries of His people, and that He intervenes in human history to deliver His people from affliction and redeem them from oppression.

Through retelling the story of the Exodus and symbolically reliving the events we are to feel as if *we ourselves* were just delivered from Egyptian bondage. Judaism maintains that God's act of liberation is not a one-time-only event, but an ongoing and repeated one. In the words of the *haggadah*, the text we use during the *seder* meal to retell the Exodus story, "For God did not redeem our ancestors alone, but us, as well."

Today, more and more Christians are celebrating the Passover holiday in their own way, motivated by a desire to reclaim  the Jewish roots of their Christian faith and the Jewishness of Jesus. Certainly, the links between suffering and joy, death and resurrection, are familiar to both faith traditions. And Christians, like Jews, affirm that darkness will be followed by light, oppression by redemption, and death by resurrection.

So as Jews around the world begin this week of Passover celebrations, I pray that we all will take time to reflect upon the story of Exodus, of a people brought from slavery into freedom because of a God who cared so deeply about humankind that He intervened in human history to deliver them, and how that redemption story is played out in our own lives.

Day 6
ATTITUDE OF SERVITUDE

Then the LORD said to Moses, "Go to Pharaoh and say to him, 'This is what the LORD, the God of the Hebrews, says, "Let my people go, so that they may worship me."'" — EXODUS 9:1

The *Torah* reading for today is from Numbers 9:1–15 and Numbers 28:19–25.

"*Let my people go*" is probably the most famous line in the entire Exodus story. God, via Moses, commands Pharaoh to let the people of Israel leave Egypt. However "*let my people go*" is only half of the line, and it represents only half of the story.

The rest of the verse reads *"so that they may worship me."* God wants the Israelites to be freed … so that they can become servants to Him! The New King James Version actually translates this verse as *"Let My people go, that they may serve Me."* Then why is Passover celebrated as the holiday of freedom when the whole point of leaving Egypt was for the Israelites to become slaves once more?

Let's take a closer look at this concept of slavery and freedom. What is slavery? Slavery means living a life without choices. You are not the master of your own life. Someone else is. Someone else tells you what to do and when to do it. You have no choice but to obey.

What is freedom? Freedom is the chance to choose your own life. You get to decide how you spend your time, your money, and your energy. It's all up to you.

Now here's the key. A person can be physically free and yet still live completely in bondage. Pharaohs come in all shapes and sizes today. Slavery is alive and well.

If your phone bings to let you know that a text has come in, and you know you should ignore it because you are in the middle of a real conversation, *but you can't* – that's slavery. If you can't resist the piece of chocolate cake even though you know it's bad for you – that's slavery. Need to have the latest fashion? Slavery. Can't help but snap at your spouse? Slavery.

Every time you go on autopilot, every-where you don't make conscious decisions, you experience slavery. The Exodus story is not just about a bunch of Jews in ancient Egypt. Every human being experiences slavery. Yet we can all experience redemption. Here's how.

No one can tell me what to do when I only listen to The One. Nothing can force me to do anything when I only do what He tells me to do. And what does God tell us to do? He tells us to rise above money. He teaches us to transcend popular opinion. He asks us to become masters of our desires. Everything that we do in service of God puts choice back in our hands. That, my friends, is why only a servant of God is truly free.

Celebrate freedom by exercising it! Before every decision you make today, ask yourself who is calling the shots. Is it the servant of God or the servant of Pharaoh? Choose accordingly.

The Egyptians Urge Moses to Depart, *by Gustave Doré*

Day 7
LET MY PEOPLE GROW!

When Pharaoh let the people go, God did not lead them on the road through the Philistine country, though that was shorter. For God said, "If they face war, they might change their minds and return to Egypt." — EXODUS 13:17

The *Torah* reading for today is Exodus 13:17–15:26 and Numbers 28:19-25, and the *Haftorah* is from 2 Samuel 22:1–15.

The sages teach that if the Bible had not been given over to man, we would have learned many virtues from His creations. For example, we would have learned faithfulness from a dog. Perseverance from an ant. Creativity from a spider. While God did give us the Bible, we can still benefit from observing His wondrous creatures. Here's what we can learn from a simple crab.

Unlike most animals that grow as an entity during their lifespan, crabs, with their hard outer shells, cannot. As babies grow into older children, their organs, limbs, and facial features grow right along with them. But a crab's shell stops growing when it gets to a certain size. Crabs have to shed their outer shell in order to grow a new one. They have to leave the old behind in order to step into something new and better. Crabs teach us a powerful lesson about growing: Sometimes, in order to grow, we have to leave behind something – or many things – that no longer suit us.

Crabs instinctively know this truth about growing. They know that without letting go of their old shell, they'll never grow a new and improved one. But as human beings, we tend to resist change – especially when it involves leaving behind a part of us. We need to learn from the crabs and let go of the old.

Exodus 13:17 reads: *"When Pharaoh let the*

people go…" However, if we translate this verse literally from the original Hebrew, we get this: *"When Pharaoh sent the people away…"* The sages explain that when it finally came time for the Israelites to leave Egypt, they were hesitant to go. Pharaoh had to literally push them out the door!

While we may have assumed that the children of Israel would jump at the chance to escape their lives of slavery and bitterness, they didn't. In fact, four-fifths of them – about 2 million Israelites – stayed behind in Egypt! Were they crazy? No. Just afraid. Afraid of change and afraid to grow.

The reaction of the Israelites to the opportunity for freedom is actually quite natural. As human beings, most of us fear the unknown. So we stay in jobs that we don't like, relationships that hurt us, or in places that no longer suit us. But there is something even scarier than the unknown: It's staying with something that we *know* is bad for us!

Passover is a time for stepping out in faith. It's a time of letting go of the old in order to make way for the new. As we shed our old selves, we can become newer, improved versions of ourselves. Pharaoh let the people go. We need to let ourselves grow!

Day 8
DANCING WITH FAITH

Then Miriam the prophet, Aaron's sister, took a timbrel in her hand, and all the women followed her, with timbrels and dancing. — EXODUS 15:20

The *Torah* reading for today is Deuteronomy 14:22–16:17 and Numbers 28:19–25, and the *Haftorah* is from Isaiah 10:32–12:6.

One of the most joyous moments in the story of the Exodus – and perhaps in the entire Bible – is the singing and rejoicing that occurred just after the children of Israel crossed the Red Sea. This was the climactic moment of what had begun as a wayward prince demanding the freedom of an oppressed people and ended with the most spectacular miracles that the world had ever seen on behalf of the downtrodden Israelites. God's hand was never so apparent, and the people rejoiced for the good that He had done for them.

Let's picture the scene: The Israelites have finished crossing the sea and they watch their Egyptian enemies getting closer. Suddenly, the sea crashes down on the entire Egyptian army! Not only are the Israelites now safe, they are also free! The Egyptians will never be able to pursue them again. Moses leads the people in a beautiful song of praise to God. Just as he finishes, his sister Miriam leads the women in song. And what's this? They are dancing and making music, too!

The question is where in the world did the women get those timbrels from in the middle of the desert? Did these instruments fall from the sky?

The sages share a beautiful explanation. They say that the Israelite women, in their great faith, prepared these instruments while in Egypt and while they were still enslaved. Led by Miriam, the women refused to give up hope that the day of salvation would come. Their faith led them to make these instruments, so that when the day came, they were ready!

Miriam's name has two meanings. It comes from the Hebrew word that means *mara*, "bitter." Miriam was born into bitter times of slavery. But the name Miriam is also related to the Hebrew word *meri*, "rebellion." Miriam rebelled against the bitterness in her life. She would not accept it — she refused to submit to hopelessness or depression. She lived her life with complete faith that the bitterness would be sweetened. And indeed it was!

Friends, it's not enough to talk about faith; we need to be willing to act on our faith. That means making life decisions based on faith in God and taking action that fits with His purposes. Our faith must be turned into actions that reflect God's Word and promises.

Perhaps it wasn't the parting of the sea that caused Miriam to dance, but rather the sea parted because Miriam began dancing way back in Egypt when she prepared for that day. Remember, while miracles have the ability to inspire faith, it also works the other way around. Our faith has the ability to inspire miracles.

THIS HOLY SEASON

The LORD is my rock, my fortress and my deliverer;
my God is my rock, in whom I take refuge,
my shield and the horn of my salvation,
my stronghold. — PSALM 18:2

Read Psalm 18.

During this holy season for both faiths, I wish my Jewish friends a blessed Passover, and to my Christian friends, a blessed Easter. In the previous devotions, I have shared with you some reflections on the Passover celebration and the lessons that can be gleaned from it for Jews and Christians alike. In fact, many of the sacred aspects of Christian worship trace their spiritual roots directly to the Jewish faith and the early history of the nation of Israel.

Such is the case with the term "Paschal Lamb," or "Lamb of God," which in the Christian tradition refers to Jesus. From the Jewish perspective, the term is *Korban Pesach*, or "sacrifice of Passover," which

dates back to the first Exodus. The blood of a sacrificed lamb, which was smeared on the doorframes of each Jewish household, served as sign of deliverance from death striking their firstborn sons. The lamb's blood would be the only path to salvation — without it, their firstborn would die, along with those of the Egyptians.

Additionally, the lamb represented the idols, or false gods, that the Egyptians worshiped. By killing a lamb, the Israelites were, in essence, defying their Egyptian masters as well as demonstrating once again the power of the God of Israel over the Egyptian gods.

In the times of the Jewish temple worship, Jews obeyed God's command to remember the first Passover by sacrificing a lamb on that day. This lamb had to be male, one year old, and most importantly, without blemish. Only then would it suffice to be the perfect Passover sacrifice. (See Exodus 12:5.)

This Passover observance is what Christians reference when speaking of *"a lamb without blemish or defect"* (1 Peter 1:19).

It is also true that Jesus, as an observant Jew, and his disciples were celebrating the Passover on the very night that he foretold his coming death. Jesus followed the same divine instructions that were given to Moses as he broke bread with his disciples. And later, the apostle Paul wrote in his first letter to the Corinthians to *"keep the Festival"* (Passover/Lord's Supper) with unleavened bread (5:8).

Indeed, the Christian observance of Easter resonates back to the story of the Jews' escape and deliverance from Egyptian bondage three thousand years ago. Understanding the story of Passover and rich symbolism of the *seder* meal gives a new richness to many of the worship traditions at churches around the world.

It is good for people of faith to remember the Jews' miraculous deliverance on that first Passover and of God's divine leading from bondage to freedom. Let us celebrate and praise along with David, in the words of Psalm 18, our rock, our fortress, and the horn of our salvation.

The Last Supper